Praise for *Be a Great Tutor*

"[F]ull of inspiring stories, ideas, and genuine help.... I plan on using these teachings techniques in my future work. [*Be a Great Tutor*] is a valuable book for tutors and teachers at a time when creative teaching and education is so important."

Dorothy Dyer, MA Architecture, University of New Mexico; MA Education, Harvard University

"*Be a Great Tutor* is as warm, encouraging, and clear in its advice as one would hope a tutor to be. I recommend this book for seasoned classroom teachers as well as for tutors who are just starting out. It offers gems for all levels of experience."

Susan Gold, MA, high school teacher

"As a principal, I found this clearly written, extremely readable, and informative book to be very helpful in guiding teachers to help our students flourish."

Sasha Clayton, MA
Principal, Hilldale S

"As a tutor, I found *Be a Great Tutor*'s practical tips to be very useful. The book provides concrete examples and strategies for many subject areas. It's worth your time!"

C. Elgersma, MFA, tutor and classroom teacher

 **Erin Quinn O'Briant** is the author of the novel *Glitter Girl*. She tutored students in a variety of subjects for many years, both privately and at City College of San Francisco. Erin has a bachelor's degree in Religion from Emory University and a Master of Fine Arts in Creative Writing from Goddard College; she is pursuing a Master of Liberal Arts at Stanford University. Erin lives near San Francisco, where she teaches writing and literature; she is also the editor of www.Tutoring-Expert.com, the companion site to this book. Learn more about her publications at www.LitBooks.net.

Contributor **Christopher Balme** is the director and co-founder of Spark, an innovative mentorship program for middle-school youth. After graduating from the University of Pennsylvania and the Wharton School of Business, Chris moved to San Francisco and founded a successful tutoring cooperative, serving youth throughout the Bay Area. In 2004, Chris co-founded Spark with fellow educator (now Spark Board member) Melia Dicker. He was honored with the Bay Area's Jefferson Award for Public Service and the prestigious Draper Richards Fellowship as well as the "Forty Under Forty" Leadership Award from the New Leaders Council. Learn more at about his organization at www.SparkProgram.org.

Be a Great Tutor

The inspiring guide

to tutoring all ages

By Erin Quinn O'Briant, MFA

www.Tutoring-Expert.com

With contributions by Christopher Balme

www.SparkProgram.org

Lit | Books

© 2011 Erin Quinn O'Briant

All rights reserved. *Be a Great Tutor* is the property of Lit Books and may not be reprinted in any form without permission.

Students' names and identifying traits have been changed to protect their privacy.

ISBN-13 978-0-984-58131-3

Library of Congress Subject Headings:

Education: General
Education: Teaching Methods & Materials — General
Education: Non-Formal Education

To all who love to learn

Table of Contents

Chapter 11: How to Be an Independent Tutor — 147

Free Tutoring-Expert.com resources for owners of *Be a Great Tutor*

Make each tutoring session a success with the up-to-date resources at www.Tutoring-Expert.com. Join our community to share success stories, connect with potential clients, download customizable documents, and much more. Free services for owners of this book include:

Your **free yearlong tutor profile** (a $20 value) online at www.Tutoring-Expert.com/profile.html. Password: tutoringsuccess. You'll have a designated page on the Tutoring Expert site and a "teaser" ad in our Independent Tutors select listing.

Access to the frequently updated **Resource Guide** at www.Tutoring-Expert.com/resource-guide.html. Password: tutoringsuccess. You'll find academic resources, online tutoring resources, and sample documents for independent tutors.

Visit www.Tutoring-Expert.com today!

Chapter 1: Introduction

A Word from the Author

Tutors, this book was written for you. When I began tutoring, I wished for a practical, easy-to-use resource with tips and advice on tutoring different ages and subjects. My friend Christopher Balme did, too, and he graciously allowed me to share his wisdom, stories, and experience in this book. I am extraordinarily grateful for his many contributions — and as you read this book, you will be, too!

Be a Great Tutor is packed with ideas from the thousands of tutoring sessions we've done, covering everything from teaching multiplication to working with adults who are returning to school. Nearly every page has a tip or trick you can use. And throughout the book, you'll find a few main themes: how to support your student with unconditional trust, build bridges between their strengths and challenges, and help them not only excel academically but feel confident in themselves as learners.

Our experience, and the findings of several academic studies[1], have shown that tutoring is one of the most effective — perhaps the most effective — approach to helping a student learn any subject, from reading to calculus. For all the teachers, parents, professional tutors and helpful friends out there, here's to your success.

Our Success Stories

Over time, a good tutor can have an enormous positive effect on a student, and this book is here to provide the practical tips you need to be a helpful, even life-changing, tutor. Of course, we've had our share of tutoring frustrations — and you'll hear about some of those. But we've offered our success stories throughout (in special font) to help inspire your tutoring practice. We'd love to hear your stories, too. Just visit www.Tutoring-Expert.com/success-stories.html to share tutoring success stories online (and grow your online presence, too).

TUTORING SUCCESS STORY: MATH

CHRIS WAS TUTORING A FOURTH-GRADE GIRL, REBECCA, WHO DESPISED MULTIPLICATION TABLES. MONTHS AGO HER CLASS HAD MASTERED THEM AND MOVED ON. BUT EVERY TIME THE CHART CAME UP, REBECCA FELT OVERWHELMED AND ANXIOUS. HER PARENTS WERE WORRIED; THEY HAD NEVER SEEN HER STRUGGLE LIKE THIS BEFORE. CHRIS ASKED HER WHAT SHE FELT WHEN SHE FIRST SAW A MULTIPLICATION TABLE: "TOO MANY NUMBERS!" SHE SAID. HE SUGGESTED TRYING A SMALL PIECE A TIME: JUST

ONE THREE-BY-THREE SECTION OF THE TABLE. THIS TIME, REBECCA DIDN'T LOOK NEARLY AS WORRIED. SHE LOOKED AT THE TABLE FOR A SECOND, AND BEGAN FILLING IN BOXES HERE AND THERE. CHUNK BY CHUNK, CHRIS AND REBECCA WENT THROUGH THE WHOLE TEN-BY-TEN TABLE, AS REBECCA'S CONFIDENCE GREW. TWO SESSIONS LATER, SHE WAS ALMOST ECSTATIC WHEN IT WAS TIME TO RETURN TO THE WHOLE TABLE: SHE FILLED IT IN WITHOUT DIFFICULTY. SHE HAD BEEN OVERWHELMED BY THE SHEER NUMBER OF NUMERALS ON A FULL TABLE, BUT WITH SOME THOUGHTFUL AND INDIVIDUALIZED TUTORING, REBECCA MASTERED THE MULTIPLICATION TABLES AND HAPPILY MOVED ALONG.

Where We're Coming From

Where do all these stories and tips come from? From real life — Erin and Chris have led thousands of tutoring sessions with dozens of students, from elementary school to adult, in subjects ranging from reading to SAT test preparation to organizational skills.

We believe in the potential of every student, and in the potential of tutors to transform learning. You do not need an advanced degree to help another person learn. Of course, basic academic skills are important. But you can share your knowledge with a student in a way that makes her want to learn, and that will help her succeed in school long after your sessions are over.

We've assembled our best practices in tutoring here to show parents, teachers, homework helpers — and, yes, tutors! — how to inspire and motivate students of all ages.

A quick note on pronouns: we're breaking the mold of current usage by using the pronoun "they" in the singular throughout this book. We also use "he" and "she" sometimes, too, when referring to students; we made these choices to avoid gender-based bias in our writing. We hope it works for you, too.

Dip in from time to time to find the specific information you need, read it through cover to cover for a general course on tutoring, or use the materials we've assembled to enrich your sessions.

TUTORING SUCCESS STORY: ENGLISH

ERIN'S STUDENT, ELLEN, WAS A SINGLE MOTHER WHO HAD FAILED ENGLISH AT A LOCAL COMMUNITY COLLEGE THREE TIMES. SHE HAD BARELY ATTENDED MIDDLE AND HIGH SCHOOL, AND DIDN'T BELIEVE SHE WOULD EVER BE ABLE TO READ OR WRITE WELL. SHE HAD MET MANY TEACHERS WHO DISCOURAGED HER FROM CONTINUING WITH SCHOOL, BUT SHE KEPT TRYING, IN PART BECAUSE SHE WANTED TO SET AN EXAMPLE FOR HER YOUNG DAUGHTER. DURING THEIR FIRST COUPLE OF SESSIONS, ERIN NOTICED THAT ELLEN PICKED UP ON NEW CONCEPTS FAIRLY EASILY AND HAD A TRUE INTEREST IN LEARNING. ERIN BEGAN WORKING WITH HER WEEKLY, NOTICING AND COMPLIMENTING ELLEN'S INTELLIGENCE, CURIOSITY, AND DRIVE.

THEN ONE DAY ELLEN BROUGHT IN A SIGN-UP SHEET FOR THE CALIFORNIA AIDS MARATHON. THEY BEGAN TALKING ABOUT ACTIVISM, AND ELLEN REVEALED THAT SHE WAS VERY CONCERNED ABOUT THE GLOBAL AIDS CRISIS AND ABOUT GENOCIDES IN AFRICA. PUTTING ASIDE ELLEN'S USUAL ENGLISH ASSIGNMENT, ERIN ASKED, "WHAT WOULD YOU REALLY LIKE TO WRITE ABOUT?" ELLEN'S EYES LIT UP. "I WANT TO WRITE TO CONGRESS ABOUT THESE THINGS," SHE SAID. "BUT I DON'T KNOW HOW."

TOGETHER, THEY LOGGED ONTO THE COMPUTER AND FOUND THE NAMES OF ELLEN'S REPRESENTATIVES IN CONGRESS. DURING THE NEXT SEVERAL

WEEKS, ELLEN WROTE A SERIES OF PASSIONATE LETTERS TO THEM AND TO BUSINESS EXECUTIVES SHARING HER CONCERNS. AFTER ERIN SHOWED HER HOW TO LOOK UP AND REQUEST LIBRARY BOOKS ONLINE, ELLEN ALSO BEGAN READING VORACIOUSLY. EACH WEEK, SHE WOULD COME IN WITH A NEW BOOK — ON RWANDA, THE HOLOCAUST, AIDS, OR GLOBALIZATION — THAT SHE WANTED TO DISCUSS. HER WRITING AND READING SKILLS IMPROVED DRAMATICALLY OVER THE FOLLOWING MONTHS, AS SHE DISCOVERED HOW HER OWN INTERESTS COULD RELATE TO SCHOOL.

Often, classroom teachers don't have time to find out about each student's personal interests — but tutors do. Encouraging students and tailoring lessons to them can lead to astonishing results.

Chapter 2: The Three Fundamentals of Tutoring

Have you ever heard a teacher say, "If you don't remember anything else I say, at least remember this..."? Well, here it is. The section with the essence of this whole book. Three techniques that build the foundation of a positive, productive, and fun tutoring experience.

#1: Meet Students Where They Are

Students spend weeks and months studying details that someone else decided they should study. What's more, they often have to study them in one way only — by sitting quietly at their desks and listening. How often are they asked, What are *you* interested in? How would *you* like to learn this material? These are powerful questions. Just asking them and listening to the answers will provide you with insight into the student's situation, and will show the students that you are interested in them.

Meeting students where they are means beginning a tutoring relationship by discovering the student's learning styles, goals, strengths, and challenges. Try gathering these pieces of information. Ask out of genuine interest, and listen carefully (maybe even take notes!):

1. What are your favorite and least favorite classes? Which subjects are easiest and which are hardest? Is that because of the teacher or the subject? If it's the teacher, what about them makes them so good/bad, easy/hard?

The answers to these questions reveal students' interests and how they respond to different types of teaching. If they love one teacher because he or she lets them write stories, that's a helpful clue for your tutoring. If they hate math but then it turns out that's because of the teacher, then you've learned that there may be an opportunity to rebuild their interest in math. Look for patterns like these in their responses.

2. How do you study material for a test? What works best for you?

Listen carefully to what students have already tried and what they feel has worked and not worked. If they've tried something and disliked it — say, they once had to make flash cards to learn vocabulary — you may be able to help them do better with it, but keep in mind there may be some resistance to it from past experience. Look for clues about the student's organizational abilities (e.g., if they say that taking notes doesn't work because they always get lost). With this and the first question, you can understand a student's general learning style and adapt it for tutoring accordingly.

3. What are your favorite hobbies? Sports? Art? Spending time with friends?

This question is an opportunity to not only discover the student's strengths, but to learn how to relate to that student. What matters to them? Is it sports, is it spending time with friends? This knowledge will help you connect with them personally and will allow you to tailor activities and exercises to their strengths and challenges.

4. When you learn something new in school, do you do best by seeing it on the board, by hearing the teacher say it, or by writing it down yourself?

This question offers more insight into the student's learning style, and offers clues about which of the multiple intelligences are strongest. For example, if a student tells you she likes to learn by taking notes, she may take in information especially well through language. A student who likes to see information in charts, graphs, or photos, may excel in spatial intelligence. When you explain a new idea to this student, try using a method that corresponds to his or her learning strengths.

5. Do you like school in general? What do you think of doing after school — what's your dream job?

This question helps you connect with the student's motivation, and reveals to what extent the student is motivated externally (e.g., "I get good grades because my parents make me," or "my parents think I should be a doctor") vs. internally ("I love English class and reading," or "I want to be an astronaut because I'm interested in outer space"). You can then include these interests in lessons, making the subject material far more meaningful and relevant to the student. For example, if a student is fascinated by outer space, you could frame a difficult math problem by involving an astronaut, or offer the possibility of a project built around studying astronauts. This helps you build a bridge between the student's interests and their challenges — as we discuss later in this chapter.

These questions and answers will begin a personal relationship and offer clues as to how to work with and motivate one particular student. And don't stop asking questions — students change continually, and it's critical that you continue to understand their motivations and interests. For example, when reviewing a completed test or paper that a student has shared with you, begin by asking them what they felt was hardest and easiest about it. Ask them where they think their strengths and weaknesses are in the subject. Then, go through the test and let the student see the logic you use to analyze it: mark down which questions were easy, and for difficult or incorrect questions, make note of which types of problems were most challenging. To have the student come up with this, we sometimes ask, "if you could go back in time and tell yourself one hint to get this question right, what would it be?" For questions they got right, ask them how they did it. As you analyze their work in this way, you respect their strengths — building confidence — and you teach them how to analyze their own work by sharing your logic with them. Then, you have a simple list of goals to work from and you know the specific issues and challenges a student is facing.

Individualize

Individualizing is what a good tutor does best. Knowing your students personally allows you to make the material relevant to them on an individual basis, like a perfectly tailored suit.

For example, Chris had a high school student once, let's call him Michael, who struggled with math. When Chris and Michael first began working together, Chris looked over some of his old tests and found that while he could often solve complex problems, there were just certain types of problems that confused him, perhaps ones that had not been covered as extensively in class. Chris spread all the old tests out on the table, and together they went through each test, going through some of the correct problems to see how he had solved them, and all of the incorrect problems to see what had gone wrong. With each type of problem, Chris either noted it down on a separate sheet of paper, or added a checkmark to an existing note. By the end they had a sheet like this:

MIKE'S (FAIRLY) EASY PROBLEMS	MIKE'S TRICKY PROBLEMS
FACTORING√	EXPONENTS RAISED TO EXPONENTS√√√√
PERCENTAGES√	CALCULATION ERROR√√√
ADDING AND SUBTRACTING EXPONENTS√√	WORD PROBLEM INVOLVING PERCENTAGES√√√√√

Along the way, they both learned a great deal about Michael's strengths and challenges, and then Chris could easily create practice problems — they called them "Mike's Classics" — that narrowed in on the specific areas where he most needed help.

Set Goals Together

As the example above shows, once you know a student's strengths and challenges in detail, and know a bit about their learning styles and interests, you can set a meaningful goal together. We don't mean something like "be a better student" — that's too general to be very meaningful. Try setting three to five specific goals, beginning with the student's suggestions. For example, one goal could be "I'll take at least a page of notes for every history chapter for the next five chapters." It's specific, helpful, and easy to measure. Another goal might be "I'll set aside 30 minutes before dinner to just do math homework."

As you may have noticed, none of these goals talk about getting a particular grade. While that often comes up, and sometimes it might end up on the goal list, "process" goals can yield better results in the long term. Grades can change sometimes with different material or a new unit in a class, even if a student is no better at the fundamentals of studying and learning. Also, putting too much focus on grades can increase anxiety and decrease the student's internal motivation to succeed academically, because the goal is no longer to understand but to get a certain letter next to their name. So, while it's fine to talk about grades and once in a while make them a goal, try focusing your goals on the underlying processes of studying — organization, study habits, and learning techniques.

#2: Build Trust and Then Listen

Define Yourself

It all starts with trust. Students have to trust you enough to share their challenges, to reflect openly about what they're good at and where they struggle, and to listen when you offer suggestions. Trust starts with your openness and your listening. To grow, it needs honesty on all sides, and that means letting the student know who you are, early on. You don't have to pretend that you are the perfect student or the teacher with all the answers. In fact, that kind of pretending will hurt the relationship because (a) no one was the perfect student and no one knows all the answers and (b) showing that you had struggles and overcame them is far more powerful.

So make sure to share a little bit about your experiences. When you ask a student those opening questions, don't just write down the answer silently — tell the student how you feel about it. If they didn't like English and you also didn't at times, tell them! If they hate math but you love math, tell them you understand but that you liked some parts of it. If they say their favorite hobby is baseball and yours is basketball, take a moment to talk about their interest and about yours. You don't need to spend long describing yourself; but make sure that the student knows a bit about you. Everyone will feel more comfortable.

What Is a Tutor, Anyway?

There's some confusion here, since students probably think of the adults in their formal education as either teachers or parents/guardians. If you aren't one of those, just what are you? And even if you are a teacher or parent, is that what you're doing now?

Try to think of it as a coaching relationship. A coach is a trustworthy person who has some experience in the subject at hand. A coach supports you to do your best, and that means cheering for you, sharing your struggles and also being honest when something isn't going well. A coach earns your respect and brings out your internal desire to perform well. We've all at times felt that a teacher is out to get us, or just to give us a grade — but a coach is always on our side, even in tough times.

Try sharing some of this with your student. And more importantly, show them why this is true. Show them that you're on their side by commiserating with a tough situation, by being honest when they're making a mistake, and by cheering them on when they have a success.

Whenever Possible, Give Options

Everyone loves options. Just the existence of options makes people think more carefully. Think of how many types of cars are available — people have to think carefully about which one they want, and they usually do! This is even more true for students, because in school they may have few options in the content or style of their learning. Think about how much of the school day is required versus how much is left open to the student's choice. Not much. So whenever you can, offer your students an option. Everything from which topic to discuss first ("Looks like we have math and English homework tonight, which would you like to start with?") to which study technique they would prefer ("I think we can get through this history chapter with either flashcards or better notes, which approach would you like to try?"). It's up to you to choose which options to offer — we'll get into that in the subject-specific chapters — but even just a few options will help your students be more engaged.

Take No For an Answer, Sometimes

The teacher or tutor always knows best, right? Wrong!
You have a lot to offer to your student, but you must be open to
the feedback they give. Say you've just realized that a student
learns best through writing, so you've asked them to take notes
on a passage in a textbook. They complain at first, but you're
confident in your approach so you ask them to try it out for a
little while. Fine. But then two sessions go by and the student still
is not learning the material any better and asks to stop doing the
notes. Time for Plan B. Tell the student that since this method
seems to not be working, at least in the time you gave it, let's
come up with a better one. Give them some options. And make
sure it's clear to them that you value their feedback, for example,
by thanking them and writing down what they said for future
reference.

How to Give Good Feedback

With younger students we often use the "feedback
hamburger" — the buns on either side offer a positive comment,
while the hamburger offers a suggestion for what to change. You
don't need to follow this approach exactly, but keep the basic
idea in mind: students (and adults, for that matter) take
constructive criticism best after they've had some positive

comments to encourage their confidence and open-mindedness. Someone who is feeling terrible because they are not confident or happy with their work will probably have trouble genuinely listening to suggestions, but someone who has recognized a strength then feels confident enough to recognize a challenge. Of course, you must make sure that your positive comments are meaningful; "good job!" is not nearly as meaningful as "I love how you described Napoleon's ambitious personality in that essay question." Not only is the second comment far more precise, but it shows the student that you've read their work carefully. Try to see that meaningful positive comments outnumber the suggestions for change.

A Note on Listening

Sometimes the most valuable advice you'll ever get is from a student's casual remark. Once, while Erin was tutoring a high school student in reading, he mentioned that the words seemed to jump out of place. It was almost as though the letters and words mixed themselves up as he read — and, of course, it was confusing. In this case, the student was eventually diagnosed with dyslexia, a learning difference that can be addressed with specific strategies. Plus, it was a relief for the student and his parents to know why he struggled with reading.

Tutoring Success Story: Reading

CHRIS ONCE HAD AN ELEMENTARY SCHOOL STUDENT WHO LOVED MATH BUT STRUGGLED WITH READING. HE WAS SO ANXIOUS ABOUT READING THAT HE REFUSED TO READ BOOKS OR ARTICLES OR ANYTHING ELSE. SO CHRIS DECIDED TO START WITH MATH. THEY DID A FEW PROBLEMS FROM THE STUDENT'S HOMEWORK, EASILY, AND CHRIS COULD SEE THAT HE WAS FEELING CONFIDENT AND STRONG, SO HE ASKED IF THEY COULD CREATE AN EXTRA-HARD MATH PROBLEM. CHRIS WROTE A FEW SENTENCES ABOUT A SUPERHERO FACING A TRICKY MATH PROBLEM. HIS STUDENT READ THE WORD PROBLEM, WITH SOME INTEREST, AND SOLVED IT. THEN CHRIS WROTE ANOTHER, AND ANOTHER. SOON, THEY HAD A STORYLINE INVOLVING A SUPERHERO AND HIS EVIL AND SNEAKY ENEMY, AND EACH DAY THE STORY ADVANCED AND SO DID THE MATH PROBLEMS. THE STUDENT WAS READING MORE AND MORE, FEELING CONFIDENT ABOUT THE MATH QUESTIONS AND FEELING THAT THE STORY WAS RELEVANT BECAUSE IT MATCHED HIS INTEREST IN SUPERHEROES. BY BUILDING THEIR FOUNDATION IN THE STRONGEST AREA — HIS MATH SKILLS — THEY HAD BUILT A BRIDGE THAT ALLOWED THIS STUDENT TO WORK THROUGH A READING CHALLENGE.

#3: Build a Bridge

If you were constructing a building, would you put the foundation in the weakest, mushiest part of the land, or would you build it on rock? Naturally you would build your foundation in the strongest possible area. With students, the same is true — begin with their strongest area and build from there. Unfortunately, some approaches focus only on the student's weakest area, leaving the student unconfident and unwilling to address challenges wholeheartedly. Instead, you can begin with a student's strength, building confidence, and then help them see connections between that strength and their challenges.

The example in the Success Story on the previous page is called a storyline, a way of helping students engage with material by creating a personally relevant story. This could work to bridge from math to reading; it could even be used to bridge from reading to math, by focusing on the story element and then gradually introducing math challenges. It could help a student engage with a social studies project by empathizing with the historical context through a story. Whatever the use, the technique works because people love stories and often learn best through story.

Project-Based Learning

Along the same lines, a student can often engage with difficult material by creating a project that is relevant to their interests. Chris once had a young student who struggled with reading and writing, but was full of all sorts of clever business ideas. He had drawn out the design for a vacuum cleaner, the greatest vacuum cleaner ever created. They spent some time drawing the vacuum cleaner together, and then began listing its features on the side of the paper — the vents, the motor, etc. Then they created a business plan for the vacuum cleaner. The student wrote down the types of people that would want to buy it, a list of all the parts it would need and how much they would cost, and wrote the text for advertisements that would appear on TV. Chris brought in some sample ads and a simplified business plan, which they read together for inspiration. All along this project — which lasted for weeks — they were writing and reading, facing this student's challenge area through a project that began with his interests.

Teaching How to Learn

No one knows everything — not even the most experienced tutor. Actually, the times when you don't know the answer are the times when your student may learn the most. Erin once tutored a high school student who was taking algebra, a subject Erin hadn't taught in a year and a half. During their first session, the student asked about a test question he'd missed, and Erin didn't know the answer. She broke into a sweat and her heart started racing, but she knew enough to be honest. "I'm not sure how to do that, so let's see if we can find a homework problem on the same topic." Sure enough, they did. In the process, Erin introduced him to an online homework help site he hadn't known how to use. By the end of the session, the student knew three things: why he'd gotten the test question wrong, that he could trust his tutor to level with him, and how to find information for himself when Erin wasn't available. He had learned how to learn.

Now that you understand the three fundamentals of tutoring, we'll apply each of them to reading, writing, math, and study skills in the next four chapters.

Top 5 Tips: The Three Fundamentals

1. Meet students where they are. Find out what your student is good at and begin your lessons where the student's foundation is strongest.

2. Build trust by telling the student what your role as tutor is and sharing your own strengths and challenges in school. Be honest, and be an ally.

3. Listen carefully to your student, and notice small comments that could signify big problems. Pay attention, and let what you learn about the student guide you as a tutor.

4. Set goals, but focus on improving process over improving grades. Yes, your student wants an A on her math test, but improving her study habits in math will improve her abilities in the long run (and probably the short run, too).

5. Teach students how to learn by demonstrating the learning process whenever possible.

Chapter 3: Spotlight on Reading

The Developmental Perspective: Getting Engaged

You probably won't persuade any students to marry their favorite book, but as a reading tutor your goal is to make them wish they could. Once students become engaged in reading and experience it as interesting, fun, and useful, they will want to continue reading, creating a positive cycle. Your own enthusiasm for reading is a great place to start. Tell your student what kinds of reading you like and how you came to enjoy it. If you struggled with reading, share that, too — it's extremely helpful for students to know that the experience of reading can change for the better.

The factors that keep students out of the positive reading cycle are wide-ranging: young children and adults who have had little schooling may struggle to learn simple words, while quite literate students sometimes "check out" when a reading gets too complicated. Nearly everyone resists being forced to spend hours reading texts they find boring, which can lead to a general distaste for all reading. Even mild learning disabilities or excessive anxiety can make reading seem too difficult to bother with — especially in comparison with easier activities, such as watching television.

Many reading tests focus on measuring a student's reading comprehension. Typically, students read a passage and then answer questions about it. The more accurate their answers, the higher the reading comprehension score. While this type of test can sometimes be useful, it doesn't measure many of the strengths and difficulties a particular student may have. Anxious students may overthink the questions, become frustrated, and simply guess. Those with limited or unusual vocabularies may answer incorrectly because they don't know a few words. And students who don't read particularly well may have learned a few test-taking tricks that artificially inflate their scores. As you can tell, you'll have to delve in one-on-one to find out exactly what each student does well and where each one needs help.

No two students read exactly alike. Think of the reading habits of people you know: some luxuriate in long novels but can't stand to wade through an instruction manual; others hoard back issues of *Wired* but have no patience for even the shortest fiction. The important thing is that the mechanical whiz is capable of reading fiction, while the novel-lover could read an instruction manual if necessary. Once students have developed a base of literacy, they can use the skill for learning and pleasure, according to their interests.

Understand the Context: Reading at Home

The value a student's family and community places on reading can be a big part of a student's success as a reader. Children who see their parents and older siblings reading for pleasure will be eager to read, too. Parents can encourage their kids to read by keeping books in the house and making regular family expeditions to the local library or bookstore. In your talks with parents, you can diplomatically suggest ways to create a "literary household" that encourages reading.

Many people don't live in communities where reading is considered a valuable skill. Erin has taught students who had to hide their books when walking home for fear of violent attack. Others don't read at home because their family members tease them. If you have a book you want to share, find out first if it would be welcome. For these students, gently suggest that there are a lot of ways to think about reading and explain why you believe it's an important, valuable skill. Be careful to avoid putting down the student's family or community — just talk about how your perspective is different and encourage your student to find a safe, quiet space for reading at school.

Whatever the particular student's home and community environment, if he is struggling to read, chances are he's faced pressure, and probably some feelings of shame, at school. If academic achievement is important to his parents, he's also getting a lot of pressure at home. Feeling singled out as a poor reader can crush anyone's self-esteem. For an adult with a low literacy level, the world can feel like a formidable obstacle course, with everything from job applications to phone bills a possible source of embarrassment and misunderstanding. Children may believe that their reading problems signal a lack of intelligence and that they won't be able to succeed in school.

You'll need help your students turn down the temperature on this pressure cooker. Let them know they can take all the time they need and that smart people struggle with reading for a lot of different reasons. Present readings at appropriate levels in small, manageable segments. Not only should readings be easy enough, they should also be age-appropriate — children's books don't work well for adults and vice versa. Let students gain full mastery over one reading before they move on to the next. If appropriate, you may want to suggest that the student's family and teachers step back while you help the student find her own motivation to become a skilled reader.

Individualize the Material and Make It Relevant

Whether they know it or not, every student wants to read something. As you get to know your student, make an effort to find out what that something is — baseball statistics, music lyrics, recipes, fairy tales, jokes, and even text messages are all fair game. People are naturally curious. Find out what your student is curious about and connect it to reading.

Suppose you have a student who loves rap and hip-hop music. Great! Whether you personally love it or hate it, rap is the poetry of popular culture. Even for skilled listeners, the lyrics can be difficult to catch, so reading a lyric sheet, and perhaps some articles about the artists and their music, can enhance the music lover's understanding. (Tip: for kids, make sure you have the "clean" version of the lyrics, and review it yourself first.) Reading music lyrics together not only creates connection between subjects, but also gives you the opportunity to slip in a little information about rhyme and meter. Tupac and Tennyson may not be so far apart, after all.

Graphic novels can be a fun, helpful resource for visual learners, especially people who love cartoons and drawing. Like comic strips, graphic novels have drawings of the action along with a written story. The main difference is that they are book-length and much more complex, with varied reading levels and content for different ages. You'll find graphic novel resources in the *Be a Great Tutor* Resource Guide online. Once you've captured a student's interest with graphic novels, create a bridge from them to un-illustrated text by encouraging the student to imagine — and maybe even draw — related scenes while he reads the words.

The most important part of reading tutoring is finding a way for student to interact with the written word. Drawings, music, activities, and games are all ways for students to find a personal connection to reading and connect it to something they already enjoy.

Tried and True Reading Instruction Strategies

These basic strategies are the foundation of most current reading instruction and are particularly helpful in helping students understand a difficult reading.

Annotation: As the student reads, ask her to highlight the important points, circle vocabulary she doesn't know, and write responses to or questions about the reading in the margin. When practiced regularly, this strategy helps students get more meaning out of each reading and makes it easier to go back and find the important points later.

Discussion: Students digest written information best when they have an opportunity to talk about what they've read. To get a discussion going, ask questions that begin with "why" and "how." An in-depth discussion about the reading gives you the chance to find out whether the student truly understands the reading and, if not, where her comprehension has gotten off track.

Pre-Reading: Sometimes diving into all the details of a text can be overwhelming, so pre-reading allows students to wade in an inch at a time. When your student gets a new reading assignment, help him understand the "big picture" first — see how long the reading is, look at the title and any subheadings, and find out who the author is. Take a look at any pictures or charts and read the captions together. Then try skimming over the first few paragraphs to see what the reading will be about. While you pre-read with your student, talk about the reading and try to predict together what the content might be.

Reading aloud: This strategy is helpful for some, but not all, students. For auditory learners, reading aloud can add to comprehension because it builds on a learning strength. Others, however, become so distracted by trying to read aloud well that they forget to notice the meaning of the words. You'll have to get to know your student to find out if reading aloud is a helpful technique or not.

Sectioning: Short readings are easier to understand than long ones. Sectioning just means breaking a long reading down into little pieces to avoid overwhelm.

Summarizing: One way to strengthen comprehension is to ask students to continually put the main ideas of the reading into their own words. You may suggest summarizing each paragraph for starters. If students have trouble writing their summaries, suggest that they put the reading away for a minute and state the main point into a recording device.

Need help convincing your students reading is important? Try these.

A few good reasons to read:

✓ Reading lets you explore the world without leaving your room.

✓ All the other kids are doing it.

✓ People who read well are more likely than others to enjoy and participate in the world around them.

✓ Literacy is one of the great achievements of humankind, and we can all participate in it.

✓ If you want a good job, a driver's license, or directions to your favorite vacation spot, you'll need to be able to read.

✓ The written word is a wide-open door to new connections and opportunities.

✓ Once you get good at it, reading is fun.

Top 5 Tips: Spotlight on Reading

1. Take the time to find out exactly which challenges your student faces; don't rely on test results alone.

2. As you work together, check for understanding. The goal of reading is comprehension, not pages consumed.

3. Keep the skill of reading in perspective and avoid shaming the student.

4. Build a bridge from a student's ability to read what interests her to what she must read for school or work.

5. Use tried-and-true reading strategies, such as annotation, sectioning, and summarizing, in the most effective way for each student.

Chapter 4: Spotlight on Writing

Understand the Developmental Perspective

Good news! Your writing students have already mastered the toughest language skill: speaking. Their speech may not be perfect, mind you, but much of your work has already been done. Everyone who can speak has a basic vocabulary and knows how to communicate through language. As a writing tutor, you're helping students take something they already know how to do — talk — and apply it in a different way. And because students can write about so many topics, you'll likely find something each student enjoys writing about.

If your tutee already likes to read, you're off to an excellent start, because reading and writing are interconnected. Students who read well are already comfortable with a reasonably broad range of words and sentence structures. They're also used to understanding ideas through language. You'll need to help these students shift from the relatively passive role of a reader to the very active, creative role of a writer. The more students read, the better their writing will be. Even ten minutes every night before bed can make a big difference over time. If your student isn't already an enthusiastic reader, though, don't despair. Chapter 3:

Spotlight on Reading is here to help; furthermore, good instruction in writing can open the doors to reading and vice versa.

Writing is not a subject that anyone learns once and for all. Even professional writers continue to struggle with finding the perfect word to express their meaning, keeping organization tight, and engaging their readers. When your students feel frustrated, remind them that writing is hard for everyone, including the people who make it look easy. There are no ultimate goals, only incremental improvements. Of course, that's all the more reason for you and your students to celebrate every accomplishment, no matter how small.

SUCCESS STORY: CONFIDENCE

ERIN'S STUDENT TYRONE THOUGHT HE COULDN'T WRITE AT ALL — HIS CONFIDENCE WAS SO LOW THAT HE WAS CONSIDERING DROPPING OUT OF SCHOOL. HIS PAPERS DID CONTAIN A LOT OF GRAMMATICAL AND SPELLING ERRORS. AS ERIN GOT TO KNOW HIM, THOUGH, SHE DISCOVERED THAT TYRONE LOVED TO ARGUE ABOUT POLITICS. HE DELIVERED SPEECHES LIKE A SEASONED LAWYER, BUT COULDN'T GET THEM DOWN ON PAPER. ERIN ENCOURAGED HIM TO TAPE RECORD HIMSELF AND THEN TRANSCRIBE THE TAPE; SHE ALSO TOOK NOTES FOR HIM WHILE HE TALKED. TYRONE WAS

AMAZED AT WHAT HE WAS ABLE TO DO WHEN HE WAS FREED FROM THE MECHANICS OF WRITING, AND BY RECOGNIZING THE SKILLS HE ALREADY HAD, HE GAINED ENOUGH CONFIDENCE TO START TO FACE THE PROBLEMS HE NEEDED TO SOLVE.

Writing Skills: What to Expect from Different Ages

Elementary School: Because young students are still building the language skills necessary for writing, we don't recommend tutoring students in the early elementary grades specifically in academic writing, such as formal essays or research papers. (Vocabulary, reading, storytelling, and handwriting, however, are some related skills a tutor can help young students master.) In fourth, fifth, and sixth grades, however, one-on-one help with sentences, paragraphs, and idea development can be helpful. Academically gifted students in this age range may be able to write basic papers, but the average student isn't there yet.

Middle School: Lots of middle school students, though not all, can write basic essays. Typically, students are familiar with most rules of grammar and sentence structure by the end of middle school. Remember the five-paragraph essay? That's what middle school students are likely learning.

High School and College: Throughout high school and college, students are learning to write increasingly complex papers, often incorporating research. They may need practice developing their ideas, incorporating outside information, and making logical connections.

Returning Adults: If you're working with adults who are returning to school, tactfully try to find out when their learning was interrupted. This will give you a clue as to what level of skill you can reasonably expect. You might ask, "Looking back on school, when do you feel you stopped learning much in class?" Many adults, especially those who grew up outside the United States, left school at an early age to begin work. Don't judge their decisions; instead, offer encouragement for what they can do now. A comment such as, "I'm impressed that you've decided to come back to school," will show the student you're on his side.

Second: Understand the Context

The more you understand about your students' strengths, challenges and interests, the easier it will be to understand why they are succeeding or struggling with their writing. Students develop difficulties with writing for many reasons. Because writing involves so many skills — everything from developing complex ideas to word processing on a computer — there are many places students can "fall down," or at least feel stuck. Start by asking your student what his strengths are; what is he good at? How is he already playing to that strength and using it to his best advantage? Follow up by asking what his weak spots are and what he has done already to try to improve. Ask if English is your student's native language, even if she has no discernible accent. Gently ask the student (or, if appropriate, the student's parents) about any known or suspected learning disabilities or differences. Also, try to get a sense of what subjects your student likes and dislikes — if your student loves math, for example, you may be able to make writing more relevant to the student by connecting it to word problems.

A writing sample is the best way see the student's challenges and strengths for yourself. Instead of reading a paper the student has already worked on, ask him to write a paragraph or two during one of your early sessions on a topic of interest to him. If your student loves baseball, have her write a page or so about the game she attended over the weekend. After she's finished writing, ask her how the experience was — did she enjoy writing it? Hate it? Something in between? The resulting conversation will likely offer useful clues for future tutoring. To avoid overwhelm, go over the writing sample together at the next session.

Remember, writing makes people feel vulnerable. Even

when the topic appears impersonal, students are putting their own ideas onto paper for someone else to read. It's a risk! When students take that risk with you, show them that they can trust you. Always comment on what they've done well and be honest but supportive about the problems.

Don't try to tackle too much at once, but instead start with a manageable goal that will give the student an experience of success. Ask students what they'd like to learn first. If their initial goal is too big — for example, they want "to write better" — guide them by asking questions that will lead them to break down the goal into bite-sized pieces. "What do you think makes a good writer?" and "If you could pick just one thing to improve, what would it be?" are questions that can help your student set a good starting goal. Students are much more interested in meeting goals they set for themselves than in goals set for them by authority figures.

When appropriate, share your own writing challenges with students. When Erin's students tell her they have writer's block, she says, "Oh, it's so frustrating! That happens to me, too." They're usually pleasantly surprised to learn that a writing teacher sometimes has trouble writing, too. Erin follows up by asking, "So, what do you do when you get stuck?" Then she discusses strategies, focusing on the student's own ideas, for getting past writer's block. She builds trust by not pretending she's perfect. Chances are, you have some relevant stories to share.

Once you've done your research on the student's particular set of needs, challenges, strengths, and interests, you're ready to tailor your tutoring to him.

Individualize the Material and Make It Relevant

What would your student love to write about? Make it a top priority in your early sessions to find a point of connection to writing — a favorite story, poem, movie, television show, or even a video game with a narrative theme. It's hard to find a kid who doesn't like stories, and even adults who don't read for pleasure often read for information or personal growth. Then use that connection as a bridge to building stronger writing skills.

SUCCESS STORY: THE INTERNAL EDITOR

WHEN PEOPLE SAY THEY HAVE WRITER'S BLOCK, THEY USUALLY MEAN THAT THEY HAVE IDEAS BUT CAN'T PUT THEM DOWN ON PAPER (OR, THESE DAYS, INTO THE COMPUTER). OFTEN, THIS IS BECAUSE OF A HYPERACTIVE "INTERNAL EDITOR" SQUELCHING THE WRITER'S FLOW OF IDEAS. NO

WRITER WOULD DARE SUGGEST EDITORS AREN'T IMPORTANT, BUT TOO MUCH NAYSAYING AT THE BEGINNING OF THE WRITING PROCESS CAN BE SELF-DEFEATING AND MAY CREATE AN INTERNAL STRUGGLE SO FRUSTRATING THAT THE WRITER SIMPLY GIVES UP. WHEN STUDENTS ARE IN THE BRAINSTORMING AND FIRST-DRAFT STAGES OF WRITING, GIVE THEM PERMISSION TO SAY ANYTHING AND MAKE ANY MISTAKE. ONCE THE WRITER HAS WORDS ON PAPER AND A GENERAL IDEA OF WHAT TO SAY, THEN IT'S TIME TO REORGANIZE. LATER IN THE WRITING PROCESS, STUDENTS CAN GO BACK AND FIX GRAMMAR, PUNCTUATION, AND SPELLING ERRORS. TRY THIS: HAVE YOUR STUDENT DRAW A PICTURE OF HER INTERNAL EDITOR — THE PERSON WHOSE VOICE SHE HEARS IN HER HEAD TELLING HER THAT HER WRITING ISN'T GOOD ENOUGH. THE PICTURE MIGHT BE ANYTHING FROM A STICK FIGURE TO AN ELABORATE PORTRAIT OF A NEWSPAPER COPY CHIEF IN A GREEN VISOR. THEN TELL YOUR STUDENT SHE GETS TO DECIDE WHAT HAPPENS TO THE EDITOR. SHE CAN PUT THE EDITOR IN THE BACK OF HER NOTEBOOK FOR SAFEKEEPING, TALK BACK TO IT, OR EVEN RIP IT TO PIECES. WHEN SHE HEARS THE INTERNAL EDITOR IN HER MIND AS SHE WRITES, SHE CAN TELL IT TO GET LOST OR ASK IT TO COME BACK LATER, WHEN SHE'S READY FOR FEEDBACK.

Good writing — even academic writing — is creative and personal (though not necessarily written in the first person). For curious, intellectually advanced students, that may be your point of connection. If you have a creative student who feels stifled by stale English assignments, you'll want to find ways to make that assignment more engaging. But some students feel overwhelmed by the complex synthesis of skills required for good writing. For them, you'll need to break down the lesson and show them the architecture behind writing.

A picture can be worth a whole paper full of words. In her study groups for college students, Erin quickly discovered that a quick sketch of basic essay structure was much more useful than verbal explanations of introductions, conclusions, body paragraphs, and where the thesis statement goes. When you draw a picture of a piece of writing, it takes some of the mystery out of the process. For overwhelmed students, practicing writing good topic sentences and plugging them into a sketch of an essay, for example, is much easier than creative writing.

SUCCESS STORIES:
JUMP-STARTING A STALLED STUDENT

IF YOU'VE GOT A STUDENT WHO'S REALLY STUCK, ASK HIM TO START A LIST OF THINGS HE HATES. YOU DON'T WANT TO SPEND TOO MUCH TIME FOCUSING ON THE NEGATIVE, BUT IT CAN GET A DIALOGUE (AND SOME WRITING) GOING. CHILDREN, IN PARTICULAR, ARE OFTEN SURROUNDED BY

ADULTS WHO BELIEVE CHILDREN HAVE NO PROBLEMS OF THEIR OWN; THESE
KIDS MAY BE DELIGHTED TO FIND AN ADULT WHO TAKES THEM SERIOUSLY.
BESIDES, YOU MIGHT DISCOVER YOU AND YOUR STUDENT HAVE MORE IN
COMMON THAN YOU REALIZED. ONE OF ERIN'S MIDDLE SCHOOL STUDENTS
WROTE A FUNNY HAIKU ABOUT PIGEONS AFTER ERIN DISCOVERED HE
DISLIKED THE BIRDS. WHEN SHE ASKED HIM LATER HOW HE FELT ABOUT
THAT SESSION, HE SAID, "IT WAS GOOD, BECAUSE NOW I'M A POET." IT WAS
A FUN EXERCISE THAT GOT HIM WRITING. SIMILARLY, CHRIS HAD A STUDENT
WHO WAS RESISTING ALL EFFORTS TO WRITE, UNTIL IT TURNED OUT THAT
HER BIRTHDAY WAS THE FOLLOWING WEEK, AND SHE NEEDED TO SEND OUT
INVITATIONS. INSTANTLY THE MOTIVATION ARRIVED, AND AS SHE WROTE THE
INVITATIONS CHRIS WAS ABLE TO COACH HER ON SENTENCE STRUCTURE,
ADJECTIVES, AND EDITING.

Once your student understands the basics, though, to keep
her interest you must continue to search for way to interest her
personally in writing. Everyone has something to say. In a
tutoring session, as opposed to a classroom, you can and should
tailor assignments to your student. Remember Ellen, the student
in Chapter 1 who discovered she could send letters to people
who could make a difference in the causes she cared about?
When her letters were finished, she wrote a research paper on
the Holocaust.

Special Section for Writing: Common Problems & Solutions

Sentence-Level Errors

The Issue: The student regularly makes mistakes in grammar, spelling, and punctuation. He may also choose inappropriate words for the meaning he wants to convey or use unconventional word order.

Solutions: Work on each issue individually, bearing in mind that too much information about mistakes can be overwhelming. Erin had a student, a bright young woman named Maria who grew up in Mexico, who had wonderful ideas to convey in her English papers but regularly mixed up verb tenses, put words in the wrong order, and made spelling mistakes (all common errors for students who learned Spanish before English). Rather than point out every problem in Maria's essay, Erin found a couple of examples of incorrect verb tense and walked Maria through ways to fix them. Then she asked Maria to find other examples of the same mistake in a different paragraph of the paper. Soon, Maria was able to find and correct her own verb errors. In later sessions, Erin used the same technique to teach Maria how to find and fix the other problems one at a time.

Tip: Many students will want you to find and fix all their mistakes. Don't fall for it! Showing students how to do it themselves takes more time and energy at first, but it sets them up for long-term success.

Confusing Organization

The Issue: Lots of students have trouble organizing their ideas so that their writing flows easily and logically from one thought to the next. Fortunately, there are fun ways to address the issue.

Solutions: 1. Rearrange. Ask your student to print out an extra copy of his paper. Together, cut out each sentence and arrange them on a colored piece of poster board. Letting the student take the lead, decide which ideas are most closely related and arrange them into paragraphs. When the student is satisfied with his arrangement, glue each sentence onto the poster board and then have him re-organize the paper based on the new arrangement.

2. *Highlight.* Using four or five different colored highlighters or crayons, have the student color-code her paper. Encourage her to choose one color for each topic, and highlight that topic in its color every time it appears, no matter where it shows up in the

paper. When she's done, she'll have a powerful visual to help her see where her organization broke down — and a road map to start fixing it.

3. *Index ideas.* If the student is in the brainstorming stage of a new writing assignment, ask him to buy a packet of different-colored index cards. You might want to have the student put related ideas on index cards of the same color; if that's too difficult, you can take the lead in helping the student decide which ideas relate to each other.

Lack of Ideas

The Issue: The student doesn't have enough to say about an assigned writing topic. *Solutions*: 1. Talk it out. Most people, especially those who haven't yet developed strong reading and writing skills, communicate ideas best through speech. Ask your student questions about the topic, and take notes on (or otherwise record) her responses. Students are often surprised to discover that they have plenty of ideas when they're not trying to put them on paper. 2. Use brainstorm maps. These are powerful but simple tools that help students get their ideas flowing. Here's an easy one to try: Have the student write the main topic of her paper in the middle of a blank page and draw a circle around it. Then have her draw lines from the middle circle. Encourage your student to scribble down all her ideas, drawing circles around them and connecting them to related ideas with lines. 3. Word blast. Sometimes a student has trouble getting started writing in general, regardless of the topic at hand. When this happens, Chris often asks his students to take a fresh sheet of paper and write for 60 seconds without stopping, while he times them. They aren't allowed to stop writing at all for those 60 seconds, even if the words don't come grammatically or in smooth flowing writing. Often this is enough to jump-start your student's writing.

No matter how good the teacher, not every assignment will inspire every student. Without saying anything negative about the assignment at hand, you can juice it up for your student by helping her discover a personal connection to the assignment or turning it into a game. If your student's head is nodding over vocabulary sheets, pull out a stopwatch and challenge her to define all the words correctly in five minutes or less. Maybe another student has been asked to write a story about something he doesn't care about. Ask him the plot of his favorite movie, then suggest creating a screenplay together instead of a story. (He can edit the screenplay into story format before he turns in the paper.)

SUCCESS STORY: WORD HOCKEY

CHRIS'S STUDENT MICHELLE HAD A KNACK FOR FUN GAMES, AND TOGETHER THEY INVENTED ONE THAT CHRIS USED TO HELP MANY OTHER STUDENTS BECOME GOOD EDITORS. CHRIS WOULD WRITE UP A SHORT STORY, FROM A FEW SENTENCES TO A FEW PARAGRAPHS, EITHER IN ADVANCE OR SPONTANEOUSLY DURING THE SESSION. IT WOULD BE SOMETHING FUNNY AND NOT SERIOUS, DEPENDING ON THE AGE OF THE STUDENT. HE WOULD PURPOSELY SPRINKLE IN ALL KINDS OF GRAMMATICAL AND SPELLING ERRORS — HUGE GLARING ONES LIKE A SENTENCE WITH TEN USELESS COMMAS, TO SUBTLE ONES, LIKE A SENTENCE THAT IS JUST BARELY A RUN-ON. HE WOULD THEN CHALLENGE MICHELLE TO SPOT AS MANY ERRORS AS SHE COULD; SHE SAID "THIS IS JUST LIKE HOCKEY AND I'M THE GOALIE — I'M TRYING TO STOP ANY ERRORS FROM SLIPPING BY!" THUS WAS BORN "WORD HOCKEY," A FUN WAY TO USE STORIES IN ORDER TO IMPROVE GRAMMAR, SPELLING, AND EDITING ABILITY.

English Teacher Jargon

As in any field, writing teachers have their own vocabulary. If you're not sure what something means, don't hesitate to ask. Here are a few common terms that can be confusing and their definitions:

ESL: English as a Second Language. This refers to students who learned another language before English. Such students often show patterns (for example, native Spanish speakers tend to have difficulty with English word order; many native speakers of Mandarin have trouble with English pronouns) that can be useful in helping them overcome difficulties.

ELL: English Language Learner. Any student who is in the process of learning English is ELL. This term includes both ESL students and people for whom English is a first language but who have not yet mastered reading and writing in English.

MLA: The Modern Language Association sets the writing style standards for English and some other subjects. When you see a reference to "MLA style," know that it's a set of guidelines that's available online or in any standard style manual. Erin routinely uses Diana Hacker's *Rules for Writers.*

Top 5 Tips: Spotlight on Writing

1. Start by focusing on the language skills your student already has, such as speaking ability, and connect those to writing.

2. Find out about your student's likes and dislikes, and then use her interests to show her why writing is fun. Tailor each lesson to your student's interests and goals.

3. Make sure your tutoring is appropriate to the student's developmental level. For example, don't expect a major research paper from a middle school child or a returning adult who left school at age 10. Likewise, don't be afraid to challenge advanced students.

4. Fix problems one at a time and be careful not to overwhelm your student with too much feedback all at once. Good constructive feedback always includes positive comments.

5. Use games, problem-solving challenges, and your own creative activities to make tutoring enjoyable and help students overcome writers' block.

Chapter 5: Spotlight on Math

The Math Context: "Math Phobia"

"Math phobia" abounds. In many parts of the world, when a student says she doesn't like math, parents — and even some teachers — likely nod and roll their eyes in agreement. Obviously, this doesn't set math students or teachers up for success. Girls, in particular, are not "supposed to" like math and may find that success in math or sciences leaves them socially outcast. (Even today, Erin encounters dismayed confusion among colleagues if she, an English instructor, mentions that she liked math in school. Most of her colleagues hated it.) This "phobia" may make your job tougher than that of many other tutors. Don't despair!

The good news is that — as you probably already know — math really is fun and relevant to real life. Your challenge as a tutor is to reveal that to your students.

Talking About Math

Whenever you talk about math with students, reveal your natural enthusiasm for the subject and be clear with students and parents about how math instruction works. Math is different from other subjects in one key way: it is almost entirely cumulative. This has an upside: a student who is failing math may actually be pretty good at identifying patterns and understanding systems — that is, with a little help that student may be able to excel in math. Missing one crucial skill (say, long division) could cripple a student throughout future mathematics classes, but finding that missing skill and learning it could save the day. More commonly, though, *not* learning one skill means missing nearly everything taught in math class thereafter. Students may head into a downward spiral quickly, and may be too ashamed to say so until tests and report cards reveal the problem. When discussing math tutoring with students and parents, explain the cumulative nature of the subject. You may want to tell them that math is, fundamentally, a "language" that reveals patterns — and it's a language than can be taught and learned successfully. Listen carefully to the problems they describe, but don't be satisfied with the information parents and students give you.

When tutoring math, be especially vigilant about finding out what the student can do successfully and where she needs instruction. Spend time going over old tests together, identifying times the student "fell down" and keeping a record of them. Don't just check off types of problems missed. Instead, take the time to find out what went wrong on each problem. Your early sessions with a math student may require frequent back-ups as you discover a missing piece of information that needs clarification.

In addition to finding out what the student knows, you'll also need to know what she cares about in order to make math relevant. Using the strategies in Chapter 2, find out which of your student's interests connect to math and plan your sessions accordingly. During your preparation time, have fun brainstorming ways math connects to the subjects your student enjoys. Your enthusiasm will be apparent during your next session.

Lastly, make sure you know the math you're teaching. You may be an ace in statistics but unable to help with basics of algebra, or vice versa. Communicate about this with students and parents to make sure you're the right tutor for the job.

Individualize the Material and Make It Relevant

Once you've identified the student's interests, you're ready to make the material relevant and to show how math can be meaningful to the student. But how? Use your imagination. Math is used in all sorts of interesting subjects — architecture, computer programming and design, art, music, video games, auto mechanics, cooking, and much more. As much as possible, engage math students in kinesthetic (hands-on) math learning. Even small tricks, such as slicing a bagel or pizza to show how fractions work, can make a difference, and that's the personally tailored instruction that tutors are well-positioned to offer. Word problems that are part of storylines may appeal to literature lovers, for example, and a student's illustrations may reach the art-inclined. Recipes make an excellent fractions lesson, so making cookies together while discussing the measurements could be a memorable (and tasty) way to get your points across.

Coping with Math Anxiety

Math anxiety is extremely common, and many students develop fear about mathematics because the subject is cumulative. If they miss one bit of math early on — say, their multiplication tables — everything else they learn afterwards will be a bit hazy. Eventually, math comes to seem totally confusing and the student starts to believe she can't do math. It can be debilitating. They key is to separate out the two issues: math and anxiety.

Handle the Math

As a tutor, you'll be able to handle the math by combining your subject matter knowledge with the techniques in this book. Remember to reduce anxiety as much as possible (see Chapter 7) by explaining math patiently, helping students set up study plans to master math skills and prepare for tests, and reminding your student that math anxiety is common — even among people who later become good at math.

Deal with the Anxiety

A little bit of tension can boost brain function, but too much anxiety shuts down the parts of the brain that we use for math, critical thinking, and similar skills. Math student sometimes become even more confused because anxiety takes over their cognitive abilities. They literally can't think.

Students learn a lot better when they know how to cope with their stress. Here are some ideas:

• Breathe deeply, making the inhale (count 1, 2, 3, 4) half the length of the exhale (1, 2, 3, 4, 5, 6, 7, 8). Try it for a few minutes. Erin uses this routinely both in tutoring and classroom instruction, and it works amazingly well.

• Exercise before tackling math problems. A few jumping jacks can do wonders. You might ask your student to shoot a few hoops before your session so she is calm and ready to learn.

• If a student can't overcome his anxiety about math, you might gently suggest to his parents that they check in with his physician. Doctors may sometimes prescribe short-term medications for anxiety relief.

Online Resources for Math Tutoring

The Internet offers an amazing array of math instruction videos. We've compiled some favorites in the Resource Guide online. Use it for inspiration and instructional assistance.

Top 5 Tips: Spotlight on Math

1. Address "math phobia" constructively and communicate your enthusiasm for the subject.

2. Spend the time necessary to find out what your student already knows and what math skills she needs to develop.

3. Find out what interests your student, then make math relevant for him. Use your imagination to connect math to interesting subjects such as stories, video games, cars, architecture, music, and more.

4. Whenever possible, find ways to help your student learn math kinesthetically — with activities and tangible objects that make concepts clear.

5. If needed, address math anxiety with anxiety management techniques such as deep breathing and exercise.

Chapter 6: Spotlight on Study and Organizational Skills

Jennifer opened up her binder and immediately a flood of notes, packets, quizzes and other papers poured onto the floor. She laughed, and Chris knew he had some work to do — here was a student who was motivated to study but had not learned how to organize her materials or her studying. They began with the binder, tossing out dozens of papers that were no longer needed and organizing the rest, with a system of folders and tabs that Jennifer created with some coaching from Chris. Next, they turned their attention to the tests and reports due that semester, and created a master study schedule, working their way backwards from each major requirement to account for all the smaller goals leading up to it. By the time they were done, Jennifer knew how to find things easily, knew exactly what she needed to study and when, and felt relieved that she could prepare for what was being asked of her. The binder looked relieved, too.

Helping your students learn how to organize themselves and structure their studying is perhaps the most important skill you can offer them. In this chapter we'll talk about several methods you can use to help your students plan carefully, set and stick to personal goals, and remain organized throughout the process. The key is to make these skills relevant, weaving them into whatever tasks or challenges your student is facing at the moment. By introducing techniques when they're most needed, you'll help your student immediately see how useful and empowering they are. We'll start with perhaps the most common study challenge.

Remembering Things

Think how often students are asked to remember things: class schedules, homework assignments, historical information, storylines from books, mathematical equations, you name it. It's enough to overwhelm the most determined memorizer. But, think of how much information you memorize without trying to — silly facts about your friends, subtle tricks to produce your favorite recipe, or tiny details from important events like a graduation or marriage.

These facts stick for two reasons: first, chances are you have either an emotional connection to them or you thought about them deeply. (You remember laughing uncontrollably at something your friend did, or you thought long and hard for months about every detail of your wedding). Second: because you have that connection or interest, you think back on these things from time to time. You remember that secret ingredient while you're cooking another dish, and that makes you think of your favorite recipe; or a friend gets married, and you think back to your wedding and all the little details involved.

In a nutshell, this means you need depth and repetition for long-term retention of information. Your students will remember things when they have an emotional or intellectual connection (depth), *and* when the topic is connected to other things in their mind, causing them to think back on it from time to time (repetition). This is our first and most important memory important technique:

Memory Trick #1:
Depth & Repetition

As mentioned above, the basis of memorizing can be summed up with depth and repetition: use your mind to think about the piece of information and process it deeply (depth), and do that frequently (repetition). Say your student has to memorize the dates and places of the 10 most important battles of World War II. How on earth do they go about remembering that?

First, help your student connect with the topic. If it's just a list of battles and dates and they don't see any connection to their lives, it's likely to go in one ear and out the other. Sure, you may ask, but how do World War II battles connect to the life of a 15-year-old student sitting in front of me? In this case, they connect because the battles tell a human story, and stories are a universal way of storing and sharing information.

Let's be more specific: first, you need to know a few things about your student. Does she prefer to communicate by telling stories aloud or by writing, or perhaps by drawing; does she tend to be more extroverted or introverted? What are her hobbies and interests? Ask genuinely and listen carefully. Say that in this case, the student loves to tell stories and is very outgoing.

Together, you can create a story that connects the people and groups that created each battle in the series. Help your student weave each event into a larger story and see how one connects to another; figure out why one battle led to another. Mention some of the personalities — what was this general like, why did one prevail over the other? Toss in a few unusual or interesting facts about each, things that will probably never be on the test. As your student's mind forms dozens of small connections within the story, they'll begin to see each event from several angles — they'll know that the Allies could not have attacked Paris until they attacked Normandy, because they came to Paris through Normandy; they'll remember the personalities and generals who were involved in several battles each. Talk through this with your students, asking them about the generals, about how each piece of the story connects. Now they're gaining depth; they've thoroughly processed the information.

Second, you need repetition: as the story creates new connections in your student's mind, keep those connections alive by regularly talking or writing about the topic. Suggest that your student talk to a study partner or friend about the events, walking through the battles chronologically as they share some of the context or perhaps unusual facts about each. When the test appears, they'll find that naming the battles and dates is as easy as telling a story they know well.

Using Flash Cards

"Flash cards" are usually 3" by 5" index cards, with a topic or question on one side, and the answer or details on the other. Not all students take to flashcards, but some, in particular those who enjoy writing or tend to learn visually, find them very helpful. They can be such a great help, especially in studies that require significant memorizing, that it's worth at least trying them with every student in that situation. Here are three quick tips to make the most of them:

Use the cards as an opportunity to have your student summarize and condense information — a major concept or event should be summed up in at most a few sentences on the back of the card (and if it just won't fit, you'll need to split it into a few smaller concepts over several cards). The thinking that is required for summarizing guarantees that your student ponders the topic carefully, which in turn helps to ensure they'll remember it. Your student should be the one writing the cards, both to make sure they've thought about the material, and to make sure it comes out in their words.

Once the cards are made, you can always cycle through the stack of cards, asking for the information on the back of each one, but creating some variations on this will keep things more lively. One of Chris' favorite techniques is to draw two cards at random from the pile and ask the student to talk about how the two concepts or pieces of information are related. After both remembering information and connecting it, students are much more likely to remember that information later.

To make sure your student zeros in on the hardest cards, try drawing a little box on the front of each card, where the single word or phrase is. When a student answers the card correctly, they fill in half of the box and put it back at the bottom of the deck. When they answer it correctly again, they fill in the other half and it can leave the deck, allowing them to gradually narrow their focus to the more challenging cards.

Memory Trick #2:
The Facts and Just the Facts!

We know that you don't always have time to create a story or study information for several days. Sometimes, you have to find a quick way to help a student gather information in their mind. Short-term "cramming" isn't a great solution, because most of it ends up getting forgotten shortly after the test, but we know that sometimes time is short. Just for this special situation, here are a few tricks.

Mnemonics

What on earth is a mnemonic? Simply put, it's a mental technique that helps you remember something. For example, when a company tells you their phone number is 1-800-WETUTOR, that's a mnemonic — they didn't think you would remember 1-800-392-1923, but by turning it into a word they hoped it would stick in your mind. In just the same way, you can convert difficult-to-remember information into a simpler, more memorable form. Here are two easy ways:

Acronyms & Reminders

We often have students trying to remember the order of operations in math: Parentheses, Exponents, Multiplication, Division, Addition, Subtraction. That can be a lot to remember. First, it is often made into an acronym - PEMDAS - which is a simple form of a mnemonic. To make it even more memorable, turn the acronym into a memorable sentence where each word matches the first letter of the acronym: Please Excuse My Dear Aunt Sally.

Create a Rhyme, Song or Short Story

Just think how much the alphabet song helped you — how else could everyone remember 26 brand-new letters? This is an example of a simple song (with a little rhyme thrown in) that helps information "stick" in your mind. Help your student create something similar, and if it sounds a little funny, that might actually help it stick.

Memory Trick #3: It's All in the Notes

Chris once had a ninth-grade student, Matthew, who loved history but was doing abysmally on tests. A quick investigation revealed some important clues: Matthew's binder contained virtually no notes, and a peek into his backpack revealed a stew of half-crushed papers, food wrappers, and unknown items lost (almost) forever. It was clear to Chris that the challenge would be to help Matthew learn how to structure and retain information.

They began with a passage from a textbook, and Chris asked Matthew to show how he would normally take notes. Matthew read the page, jotted down one word to sum it up on his notepad, and moved right along to the next page. "Wait!" Chris asked him to pause, and asked, "If I came back to you in a week and showed you that word, could you summarize what was on that page?" Matthew had to admit that he would not be able to. Chris then worked with him through the page, asking him with every paragraph, "What is the most important thing in this paragraph? If you had to sum it up, what would you say?" Often, Matthew would still pick out a detail that was too small; each time that happened, Chris asked him to look again or suggested an alternative. After practicing together like this, Matthew began to see that most paragraphs could be compressed into one good summary sentence. To do this, Matthew was not only reading the material, but having to think carefully about it — providing the depth needed to retain information.

But our story isn't over just yet. At the end of a chapter, Matthew had a *lot* of notes. What was he supposed to do with these? Chris showed him a technique called Generations of Notes — it's a way to squeeze more information into a smaller and smaller space, until a few sentences can truly remind you of a long passage. Not because they're the world's longest or most amazing sentences, but because of all the careful thinking that went into each one. So, once the chapter was done, Chris asked Matthew to take notes on his notes. "What?!" was the reply. Chris showed Matthew how each page of his notes could be condensed even more, into a few paragraphs of notes — he called these the "Second Generation," since the First Generation were the original notes.

This isn't easy, since the First Generation was already a shorter version of the chapter itself. But by thinking carefully about what was needed and what could go, Matthew got to know the material very well. By the time he was done, he had the ideal study sheet, and he knew the information well. With a good study plan, Matthew had a friend quiz him based on the study sheet, and before long he knew the material cold. If you need to, you can even do three generations of notes to get to this stage. Remember, it's all in the process, which leads the student to think deeply and often about the topic.

Make It Personal

The more you know about your student — what their hobbies and interests are, how they communicate, what makes them laugh — the better you'll be at suggesting the right learning technique, and the more you can weave together schoolwork with their personal interests. Imagine a student who loves art and is preparing for a difficult science exam, with many related concepts they must memorize. Knowing that they love art, you might pull out a large piece of paper and some markers, and together create a beautiful, visual representation of the information. Perhaps that means writing down main ideas, turning them into bubbles, and connecting them with links that show their relationship. Chris once did this with sidewalk chalk on a driveway, helping a very visually-oriented student master the process of photosynthesis for a high-school biology class. They had fun drawing out the process and even walking from one bubble to the next as the student described how it worked. Chris' student later said that she could remember the whole driveway and even the different colors of chalk, and she aced the test, much to her surprise.

Helping Your Student Get Organized

You've probably encountered the famous Messy Student. This student may have one or more of the following: a binder that appears to have been run over by several large vehicles: a desk that was unfortunately involved in a recent hurricane; or best yet, the backpack that is both a refrigerator and a trash can. All right, we admit that one or more of these may have applied to us. But the truth is, many wonderful students run aground because of poor organization, even if they have the ability to easily master the topic at hand.

To see what you as a tutor can do about this, begin by observing and asking a few questions. You're the detective here; ask the student what they usually do when they receive a piece of paper, or are given an assignment. How and where do they usually work? Do they have one organization system for topics they really love, and another for topics they don't like? Take a peek into the backpack and the binder or other papers. After gathering some information, you'll be ready to select one or more of these tricks to help your student.

Showing Why Organization Helps

Organization can certainly seem like a chore, especially when someone is asking you to organize. Depending on the student, a few questions could show them, directly, why organization is helpful. Give them a challenge: how quickly can you tell me the date of your next math test? How quickly can you find the science quiz you took three weeks ago? Challenge your student to decrease their time, no matter what paper they're looking for, by creating a strong organization system. Plus, you can point out that the less time they have to spend searching for things, the more time they have later to do whatever they want.

Organization Trick #1: Own It!

If a binder or book is being treated roughly, that's often a sign that the student feels it's not relevant, interesting, or important to them. There are other ways, as described, to build a bridge between a student's interest and a given topic, helping them connect with it personally. In terms of organizing, it helps to have the student feel a sense of personal ownership of their materials and work space. There are some simple ways to do this: for younger students, you may want to decorate a binder, book cover or even backpack together, making it distinctive and more personal. For older students, help them develop a system of files, folders, and/or tabs together, and make sure to base it around however they divide the topic in their mind.

If they aren't already using a binder, that's a great way to begin — a binder allows you to divide topics into folders and tabs, and multiple binders can do this across several topics. Investing in a good three-hole punch means that any paper can be filed away neatly within the binder. The key here is to make sure the organizing system makes sense to the student; perhaps they'll want to store their homework in one folder, covering all the different subjects, or perhaps they'll store each piece of homework separately. As long as they know where to find things easily, it works.

These rules apply to your student's personal study space as well; whatever they have, whether a full desk or part of a kitchen table, make it as personalized as possible. If they're sharing a space and have to frequently move their things, suggest that they buy a small box or file crate to be able to move papers and materials without losing organization. If it's a full desk, ask what type of space makes them feel most focused — do they want a totally clear desk, or can a few organized files sit on the side? Help them ask questions of themselves about what kind of space works best, and then all you need to do is gently remind them of the goals and conditions they set for themselves.

Organization Trick #2: Goal-Setting

One of the greatest gifts you can give your students is to help them master goal-setting: how to set out positive future goals, build a structure to achieve them, and know how to get support and make changes when needed. Chris is a big fan of "Backwards Planning." Start with your goal — say, completing a 10-page research paper — and then gradually work your way backwards toward the starting point, setting smaller goals along the way. You might start by saying that a week before you turn it in, you'll need to have the rough draft done, to give you time to review and share it with peer editors. A week before that, you'll need to have the outline ready; two weeks before that, you'll need some time in the library to gather information; and so on. Eventually, you have a series of clear steps, each with a small goal (e.g. "Complete two-page detailed outline") and a date. Then you know exactly when you need to start and how long the whole process should take. The more you do this, the better you'll get at estimating time. As a tutor, you can be of great help to your student by helping them to create reasonable time estimates, something that is often challenging for those still getting used to this kind of planning.

Accountability

Goal-setting depends on accountability: you have to have faith that the goals will be completed and that others care about it. In turn, accountability depends on personal commitment: if a goal is forced on you, you may ignore it, but if you create it yourself, you'll naturally feel committed.

Combine these two, and the simplest way to create accountability is to coach your student to create their own list of goals, and then ask them to share it with others. After setting goals, it's helpful to ask your student to share them with family, teachers or friends, as well as with you, of course. Publicly stating their goals will likely help them feel more committed. Imagine that you signed up for a new gym membership and told all of your friends that you would go at least three days a week. On that day when you don't feel like going, you'll be much more motivated by knowing that someone will ask you about it the next day.

Once the goals are set, every time you meet, ask your student to give you a brief update, or check in with them briefly on individual goals: "How is everything going with the research paper? I see you had expected to be done with the outline by this week; how did that go? Did any questions come up that I can help with?" With some students, especially middle school or younger, Chris sets up visual systems to represent the goal — often a bar chart that's filled in a bit more each time progress is made.

Asking parents to sign off on the achievement of certain milestones can be another way to create accountability. The key with this is that the student helped to create the goals and the structure — that way the accountability is natural, not something they might feel was forced upon them.

By consistently showing how to set goals, and sharing how you personally set your own goals, you can help a student shift to a longer-term perspective about their work and their plans. For many students, this is a huge relief. Not knowing when they should begin working on something means that they feel the weight of their future work right now; with some planning and practice, they'll know when and for how long they need to work.

STUDENT SUCCESS:

THE RIGHT STUFF, THE WRONG STUFF

THROWING THINGS AWAY CAN BE THE MOST FUN AND USEFUL WAY TO BEGIN ORGANIZING. IF YOU SUSPECT YOUR STUDENT HAS STUFFED TOO MUCH INTO THEIR BACKPACK, BINDER OR FOLDERS, SET SOME TIME ASIDE TO LOOK THROUGH IT TOGETHER. ASK THEM IF THEY NEED EACH PAPER FOR A PARTICULAR CLASS, OR IF THEY MIGHT USE THE INFORMATION ON IT FOR A FUTURE PROJECT. SOME CAN PROBABLY BE THROWN AWAY IMMEDIATELY, AND IF YOU'RE NOT SURE IF AN ITEM MAY BE NEEDED LATER, HELP YOUR STUDENT CREATE AN "ARCHIVE" OF OLD PAPERS. THIS CAN BE A SMALL FILING CABINET, A BOX WITH FILES IN IT, OR EVEN A LARGE BINDER — AS LONG AS IT DOESN'T HAVE TO BE CARRIED AROUND EACH DAY AND HAS ITS OWN ORGANIZATION SYSTEM. THE LESS THEY HAVE IN THEIR BACKPACK OR FOLDERS, THE EASIER TO FIND WHAT THEY REALLY NEED WHEN THEY NEED IT.

Organization Trick #3: Managing Time

Life is full of distractions, and that's especially true at school — friends, teachers, homework and more are vying for each student's attention. Often, when students come home, they want to be as far away from bells and schedules as possible. But if you can help your student create their own time management style and system, they're much more likely to follow through with their goals, and they'll feel more productive and in control of their time. Here are a few keys:

Find their ideal conditions: Ask your student to tell you about times when they have felt very focused and productive. Is it better in the morning or evening; when there are others around or when they are alone; with music in the background or silence? Help them realize that all of this is valuable information that can be used to create ideal study situations. Knowing what time of day you work best in means you know just when to do your highest-priority tasks.

Monthly view: For students in middle school and higher, help them plot out their assignments and other priorities on a scale of several months. This may seem like a long time, or may require more information than they have on hand, but as much as possible, help them shift into this longer-term perspective. Then, as they spread goals out across the calendar (see backwards planning), they can create daily to-do lists. Finally, make sure that they are prioritizing these lists at least once per day, as described below.

Prioritizing: Help your student develop a habit of regularly asking themselves what is most important for them to be doing, and what is most urgent. Tasks that are both important and urgent should be done right away; tasks that are just important, or just urgent, should be prioritized in rough order. They could either make a list in order of priority, or have a simple system, for example assigning an A, B, or C to each item to represent how important it is: A means get it done today, B means it's important, C means get to when you can.

Handling distraction: You may want to suggest that your student carry a small notepad with them for random ideas and thoughts that pop into their head; whenever they appear, if the student is in the middle of doing something else, they can write them down on the pad. That way the student can return to their topic knowing that the idea will not vanish.

Top 6 Tips: Spotlight on Study and Organizational Skills

1. The more you listen to and learn about your student, the more you'll be able to help them connect information to their interests, create stories that help them remember things, and develop an organizational system that suits their style.

2. To help your tutee remember just about anything, create opportunities for them to think about the material carefully (depth), and then with stories or other connectors, help your student think about it often (repetition).

3. Show your student how to take excellent notes, summarizing and organizing information as they go. They'll gain a lifelong study skill and will improve their ability to retain information.

4. Help your student feel a sense of ownership over their materials and binders, personalizing them as much as they can, and coach them to make a system of folders or tabs that matches how they mentally organize information.

5. Take the long-term view in planning — show your student how start with final goals and work backward to include all the steps needed along the way. Once they have a plan, help them learn to manage their time by asking them to set dates and/or time estimates for each step.

6. Whenever possible, goals should be set by the student

and then shared with others. The more the goals come from the student, the more invested they'll feel and the better they'll be at following through.

Chapter 7: Testing, Testing

In an ideal world, students would look forward to a test because they want to know how to improve or they want to measure themselves against a known standard of excellence. Unfortunately, that motivation usually happens only when students choose to measure themselves, and how often do students choose to take a test? As a result, few areas of study contain more stress and fear than testing — and few areas contain more potential for dramatic improvement with a tutor's help. Not only can you offer powerful study techniques, but you can help your student see the test as a personal challenge, almost a game, that they have the tools to overcome.

Imagine that you received a letter stating that in one week, an official examiner will visit your home and will measure your personal ability to keep a "nice" home. He will rate you on a 20 point scale, and if you score 10 or lower, you will be immediately asked to leave your home; if you score between a 10 and 15, you'll have two days to make the changes he suggests. If that was all you knew, you would likely be terrified — how on earth will he grade you, what will he look at, how can you prepare? This is how so many students feel with a test, whether it is a fifth grade math quiz or a college entrance exam. Imagine, instead, if the letter had a second sheet with it that said: You will receive 5 points if there is food in the refrigerator, 5 points if the lights work, 5 points if you say hello at the door, and 5 points if the plants are watered. Now, you can relax: you know just what you need to do, and it's almost a game to make sure that you get all the points you need. This is what you as a tutor can offer: help your student figure out a roadmap that shows just what they need to do to succeed on a test. Break it into bite-size pieces, offer tools allow the way (see Chapter 6: Study & Organizational Skills), and tests will no longer be confusing, insurmountable obstacles.

There's one more benefit to taking the fear out of tests: they will be less likely to get in the way of your students' personal enjoyment of education. Often, students' whole view of school is focused on tests and papers, and they forget the natural joy in building one's knowledge and awareness of the world. By helping your students understand the tests and organize themselves for success, as we describe here, you may just make a huge difference in how much pleasure they take in their education.

Conquering Test Anxiety: Tutor Strategies

Chris once had a student named Jocelyn who noticed a strange effect when it came to testing. They would do a math quiz together in Jocelyn's home, and she would confidently answer nearly every question correctly. But the next day, looking a little ashamed, Jocelyn would bring home a very similar in-school math quiz, with half the questions wrong. After this happened twice, Chris realized that the problem wasn't so much about the material itself. He asked Jocelyn to describe the situation and her feelings when she was taking a test in class. She said she felt nervous beforehand, that she tried to take the test as quickly as possible and was the first one to turn it in; that she was distracted by how quickly the other students seemed to be going through the test. She was confused and a little scared, not sure why she was forgetting important information during the test. She was starting to say things like "I hate math" even though Chris knew she had a strong natural ability in mathematics.

Chris got to work: he began by sharing some of his own experiences with stressful tests, making sure that Jocelyn knew she was not alone in feeling this way. Then he said that he had gotten past that stress with a few techniques:

Concentration: He asked Jocelyn if she could, as soon as she received the test paper, take a long, deep breath and remind herself of how well she had done on the practice test. If she found herself starting to breathe faster or getting anxious during the test, Chris asked her to pause and take at least 10 seconds on one single deep breath. If she had a recurring thought that wouldn't leave her mind, Chris suggested that she jot it down quickly on a piece of paper, and then let it go from her mind.

Pacing: If you want to do as well as possible, you may as well put all the time you have available to use for the test. They did a practice quiz, with Chris timing it, and came up with an average time for each question: it turned out to be roughly 30 seconds per question. Chris didn't want Jocelyn to be glued to the clock, so he asked her to set a few check-in points — after question 10 she should be around 6 minutes into the quiz, and so on. If she was running ahead, she could tell herself to slow down slightly. If she was running behind, she knew to try not to waste time on distractions or especially tricky questions.

Preparation: In this case, Jocelyn was preparing well with practice questions. But sometimes, students who are trying to cram information before a test can become very anxious, since their hold on the information is not very strong. In those cases, better preparation can be the best solution to anxiety: if the student uses techniques like "generations of notes" (See Chapter 6) to make sure they understand the material deeply and from several angles, they have less to fear from forgetting.

Expectations: Often, students hold unreasonable expectations about tests, and these expectations can disappoint or distract them from focusing their efforts. For example, many students feel that no matter what, they must try to answer every question on the test. As we'll see below, especially with standardized tests, this expectation can be a major obstacle. Sometimes it is far better to answer the questions you know how to answer, rather than run out of time answering questions you don't know and missing ones that would have been easy for you to answer.

Self-checks: Many students turn the test in as soon as they finish the last question, not wanting to check over their answers and spend any more time on the test. It's understandable that they want to be done, but help them develop a skill in self-checking. Chris always asks students to place a small check mark next to questions that they would like to come back to, and for questions that really need more help or that they skip because of lack of time, two check marks. Then, if they have time for a self-check at the end of the test, they know just where to go. With a little practice, students will see that this skill can easily win back several points that might have been lost to small mistakes along the way.

Visualization: For some students, especially those who have trouble getting past anxiety even with the techniques above, Chris runs a brief visualization exercise. He asks the students to imagine the ideal test situation: they receive a test at their desk, take a deep breath, smile and begin reading the paper. As they continue, they answer question after question confidently, occassionaly skipping one that they know would take too much time. They calmly check their work, and just before time is called, hand the test back to their teacher. Chris asks them to carefully imagine each moment, not just saying it, but imagining what it feels like to turn over the first page of the test confidently and calmly, and describing that feeling. Then, during the real test, Chris asks the students to remember that feeling. For some students, this is just the ticket to reducing anxiety during tests.

Techniques like these take some time to sink in, usually; if students have been feeling anxious with tests for some time, it may take some time for them to change their habits. However, with a patient tutor reinforcing these ideas over time, you'll see students begin to relax and improve their test-taking ability. In this case, Joceyln found the breathing exercise especially helpful, and several tests later, reported results that were closer to her practice test scores at home.

Planning to Succeed

Many students are scared of tests because they don't know how to plan and prepare for them. They realize that they need to master a certain subject on a certain date, but how are they supposed to get from here to there? Here's where you can offer them an invaluable planning skill: backwards planning. As discussed in Chapter 6, this means first understanding what exactly will be tested and how it will be tested, and then working backwards as you decide on each step that will be needed to reach your end goal. Say that your test is an essay about the novel *1984.* You might create a plan like this:

January 30: Test with essay on *1984*

January 28: Set up a study group or phone call with friends to discuss main themes from the book

January 26: Finalize your version of the outline of the plot and major characters, along with a description of major themes in the book

January 22: Write up a rough draft of a plot and character outline

January 20: Read the last few chapters of the book

January 17: Read from the middle of the book up to the last few chapters

January 14th: Make sure I've read the first half of the book

January 5: Begin reading the book, taking notes on key plot and character moments, and interesting themes or ideas as you go

Now the steps have become small, not-so-overwhelming pieces that a student can understand and imagine completing. Make sure that your student creates this plan, rather than you creating it and giving it to them; the more they put into it, the more ownership and commitment they'll feel to it.

Similarly, help students create study checklists to make sure they have everything covered. Ideally, they'll create a checklist and then run it by you; let them know how much they've covered successfully, and point out any areas they may have missed.

Fundamentals of Standardized Testing

Students face a dizzying array of standardized tests, beginning as early as elementary school and intensifying as they continue through their education. For many students, the Scholastic Aptitude Test, or SAT, which plays a key role in many colleges' admissions process, represents an especially challenging hurdle. As we've stated, this can unfortunately distract students tremendously from their natural interest in learning, but we can offer a few ways to both remove stress and improve students' scores on standardized tests. These are all in addition to the tips above, which apply at least as much to standardized tests as any other. In addition to these general tips, we also recommend investing in a test-specific preparation guide, such as those made by The Princeton Review, which will provide strategies specific to that test. Here are some general tips:

Be selective in what questions you answer: As we said above, if all questions are worth the same amount of points, make sure you answer the easy questions before the hard ones. This may sound obvious, but many students proceed through the test getting stuck on hard questions when there are easier ones just waiting to be answered. Advise your student to place a check mark next to a hard, time-consuming question and skip it, leaving time to answer the easy ones and then get back to the hard ones later. Remember, this only applies when all the questions are worth the same amount, so be sure to check that first.

Learn the test itself: Make sure your student understands how the test is scored. For example, if a multiple-choice test gives a point for every correct answer and no points off for an incorrect answer, make sure your student answers every question on the test, even if it is a wild guess, because she is bound to get some right just by luck. On the other hand, some tests deduct points for incorrect answers, meaning that she should only guess if she can first narrow down the possible choices. A computer-adaptive test (CAT) doesn't allow students to go back to unanswered questions. Instead, the computer selects future questions based on the student's answers. If a student gets the first question right, the next question will be harder; if she gets the first question wrong, the next question will be easier. As you can imagine, students sometimes drive themselves a little batty wondering if the questions are getting harder or easier.

Use a diagnostic test to find out what your student already knows and where extra studying will be most useful. You should plan a general review of all the material, but you may be able to zero in on specific types of questions. When Erin took the GRE exam for graduate school, for example, she used a diagnostic test to find out what she could do to improve her score. She found that when she made mistakes in the Verbal Reasoning section they tended to be analogy questions. She focused her studying on analogies and therefore felt confident answering those questions on the test.

Be familiar with the test: You don't want your student to be surprised by anything about the test itself — make sure she has practiced enough to be comfortable with the format, sections, and types of question asked on the test. For nearly every major standardized test, you can find practice books (often in test guides); suggest that your student spread these practice tests over the few months leading up to the test, timing themselves just as carefully as if it were the real test. Then, you and your student should carefully review the test, categorizing each incorrect answer according to the type or subject of the mistake: for example, was it a careless error, a mistake with multiplication, a mistake in recognizing run-on sentences, etc. Then you'll see just where you as a tutor should focus your efforts, and you can see if the hardest areas get better on the next practice test.

Keep in mind what is really measured by these tests. When a test says it is measuring "verbal intelligence," it may really be measuring vocabulary more than anything else, as is the case with parts of the SAT. If you think your student must master everything from "verbal intelligence" to "mathematical reasoning," it can be downright intimidating. But after reviewing some practice tests with them, you may realize that what is really needed may be just some test-taking strategy (see above), help on vocabulary, and practice in a certain few tricky types of math questions. Again, we recommend buying a test-specific study book to provide you with study suggestions that are specific to the test's format and content.

Top 5 Tips: Testing, Testing

1. Reduce fear as much as possible by encouraging your student to think of a test as a winnable game.

2. Understand the test itself, including the scoring system. Check out the Resource Guide for help selecting test-specific materials.

3. Break the study process down into bite-sized pieces, and coach your student on working backward toward the testing goal.

4. Use tried-and-true test-taking strategies such as self-checks and visualizations.

5. Refer to the study and organizational skills in Chapter 6 to help the student remain calm.

Be a Great Tutor

Chapter 7: Group Tutoring and Workshops

What's Growing in This Petri Dish?

Many students learn especially well in a small-group setting, with a few of their peers and a group leader. Tutoring groups are excellent ways for students to learn how to communicate clearly and comfortably, share ideas, and exchange feedback and support with peers. For shy people, groups can serve as a safe setting in which to learn how to speak up; for those who tend to talk too much during class, working in a group can teach them when to speak up and when to let others take the floor. For tutors, especially those running their own business, groups and workshops can boost income while giving students a lower-cost tutoring option.

If you are running a group, don't think of it as second-best to individual tutoring or classroom teaching. Think of it as an intellectual petri dish, a specially prepared area where students' social and academic skills can flourish together.

Your Role as Leader

When you begin running a group, you'll need to establish your role with your students. Sit with them instead of standing over them in the traditional classroom style, and make sure they know you are not handing out grades or sniffing around for the "best" student in the group. Do be clear, however, that you will be in charge of facilitating the group's discussions and activities, and that you'll make sure the group stays on track. Ideally, you want to cultivate a relationship with the students in which they trust you both because you are not a traditional authority figure (and are therefore safe to share insecurities and mistakes with) and because you are a responsible and knowledgeable leader.

Ongoing Study Groups

An ongoing study group format is one of the most common kinds of tutoring groups. Typically, tutors either partner with an individual teacher to provide tutoring support for a particular class or offer, say, a weekly elementary algebra tutoring group that's open to students from any class. In college, graduate student instructors or teaching assistants may facilitate study groups for students in big classes. Specific programs have varying ways of managing the process, though: for example, Erin worked in a program in which professional tutors partner with classroom instructors to provide ongoing study groups for college students taking English courses. Groups of four to ten students tend to offer a good combination of tutoring opportunities, since they're small enough that you can give each student personal attention but with the critical mass to create a group dynamic.

One of the greatest benefits of such groups for students is the opportunity to form lasting bonds with each other. Of course, a group should not be social hour. But a good group will offer chances for members to get to know each other. When appropriate, encourage students to continue studying together outside of the regular sessions, too. (A note of caution: students should only share personal information when they feel comfortable, and with a new group of students who don't yet know each other, have them meet in a public place such as the school library.) Explain that getting to know other students who share their goals is good for their academic success. Friends are a great source of moral support during tough times in school (and in other parts of life), and developing a variety of social relationships helps students build their communication skills, too. That translates into better class participation grades, more positive interactions with teachers, and higher self-esteem.

Whatever your group's particular focus, in an ongoing study group you have a special opportunity to help students develop *metacognition* — the ability to think about thinking — by letting them decide what topics they want to cover on a given day and what strategies may be most effective for them. For example, they may need help with a particular homework assignment, advice on conducting research, or an opportunity to discuss a reading. At the beginning of the group session, ask the students what they want to work on, making sure to get at least one comment from each. Then center the session on their needs and interests.

STUDENT SUCCESS:

LETTING STUDENTS SET THE AGENDA

ERIN BEGAN EVERY STUDY GROUP WITH THE QUESTION, "WHAT'S ON OUR AGENDA?" STUDENTS CALLED OUT THE TOPICS THEY WANTED TO TALK ABOUT: "LAST NIGHT'S HOMEWORK" AND "THE MIDTERM" AND "MY OUTLINE." AS THEY TALKED, ERIN WROTE EACH TOPIC ON THE BOARD. THEN, THEY ALL AGREED ON AN ORDER FOR THE DISCUSSION — OUTLINES FIRST BECAUSE THEY'RE DUE TOMORROW, PERHAPS, HOMEWORK SECOND, AND THE MIDTERM LAST BECAUSE THAT CAN BE POSTPONED UNTIL THE NEXT SESSION IF NECESSARY. ERIN USUALLY LET THE STUDENTS DECIDE THE ORDER, BUT SOMETIMES STEPPED IN TO GUIDE THEM IF THEY WERE HAVING TROUBLE.

THIS PROCESS INTIMIDATES SOME STUDENTS AT FIRST. SOMETIMES THEY FEAR THEY'LL SAY SOMETHING WRONG BUT, MORE OFTEN, THEY SIMPLY AREN'T USED TO BEING ASKED WHAT AND HOW THEY WANT TO LEARN. THEY HAVEN'T THOUGHT ABOUT IT! KEEP ASKING QUESTIONS UNTIL THEY START TO COME UP WITH IDEAS ON THEIR OWN. AFTER A FEW SESSIONS, STUDENTS ARE EAGER TO GET THEIR AGENDA ITEMS ON THE BOARD, AND ONCE THEY'VE GOT THE HANG OF IT YOU CAN LET MEMBERS OF THE GROUP HANDLE TAKING AND ORGANIZING THE AGENDA.

Preparing, Not Planning

When Erin first began running study groups, she made the understandable mistake of trying to plan activities ahead of time by anticipating what students would want to work on. She guessed wrong every time. If she walked in ready to drill on thesis statements, the students would announce that they were confused about coordinating conjunctions; if Erin planned a discussion about a reading, the students demanded to know more about thesis statements. Because Erin knew what the teacher was covering, though, she was able to adjust quickly to meet the group's needs. You can do the same by preparing yourself in general without planning exactly what will happen during the session.

Over time, Erin developed a repertoire of easy-to-implement activities that she could use when needed, and she stopped trying to anticipate (and control) the group's focus. She thought of this repertoire as her "bag of tricks," and she dipped into it, metaphorically speaking, during almost every session. Instead of planning specific lessons, she used her preparation time to think of new "tricks" to use when the time was right. (You'll find some of these in the Resource Guide.) Your best preparation is to know as much as possible about what your students are learning in their classes. Ask them to share their course syllabus or class schedule, and plan your preparation accordingly. If they're reading *To Kill a Mockingbird*, so are you. If they're doing a mock trial, you brush up on court procedure. They may or may not want to talk about it in their study group, but you can relax knowing that you're ready for the conversation should it arise.

When students bring up a new topic, don't immediately launch a dog-and-pony show on that subject. First, dig to find out what the real question is. For example, a young man named Claude came into his English class's study group and said he wanted to know how to write a conclusion — that he was stuck on his. Rather than regurgitating everything she'd ever learned about concluding paragraphs, Erin began asking questions. "What have you got so far? Have you written a good concluding paragraph before? Where exactly are you stuck?" The other students joined in with their own concerns and suggestions. As the conversation continued, Erin realized they weren't really struggling with conclusions. They were actually having trouble following the teacher's instruction to restate the thesis statement in the conclusion: the real problem was paraphrasing. From there, it was easy to ask a student to write two or three sentences on the board, practice restating them together, and have the students apply that skill to their conclusions.

Another useful way to build students' self-esteem is to build on the knowledge they already have. Even the youngest students have prior knowledge, and building on that makes it easier for them to learn. If your students claim they can't do long division, remind them of what they do know. Ask them to brainstorm everything they can remember about long division. Based on your experience with them, you could ask them to remember that they do know something: how to do simple division, for example, or how to set up the problem correctly. Ask the group to work together on the first few steps, then guide them along if they get stuck.

Think of student-centered study group tutoring as in-the-moment teaching. You can't prepare discussion questions: you don't know what the discussion will be about. What you can do, though, is ask the questions you find most interesting and relevant in the moment. Challenge the students to think about the tough questions. They will run with it. For the tutor, this is an opportunity to develop a new set of extremely valuable skills: thinking fast, creating fun lessons on the fly, and discovering how much you already know about a subject. You'll also learn how to let go of control and give some of the power over to the students.

Creating Positive Group Interactions

Whether your group is coming together for one day or an entire academic year, your first task is to help the students interact with each other in a way that is as enjoyable and useful as possible. Early on, ask them what they want to get out of being in the group. Then ask the students to suggest ways to meet those goals. You could add some of your own, too.

One way to build both trust within the group and self-esteem for individuals is to have the students share their academic strengths with each other. This can feel socially awkward, so to make it easier you can pair up students and ask them to interview each other about what they do well in school. Then have the partners take turns introducing each other and describing each other's top three academic strengths.

When the students' strengths have been described, talk

with the students about how these strengths can work together. Erin often ran groups in which about half the students had taken English as a Second Language classes and half hadn't. The ESL students were likely to have a thorough knowledge of English grammar, while native speakers usually had a strong sense of the flow of the English language and better pronunciation. In a math group, some students may be good at solving problems in their head, while others excel in drawing pictures of mathematical concepts. Such differences can divide a group unless the leader provides a context in which students can see how their differences provide opportunities to learn from each other. To nudge them along, ask students to think about and then discuss what they can learn from one another. They'll quickly come to see that their differences are often complementary.

In order for all members of the group, including the shy ones, to feel safe, you will need to establish some behavioral expectations. One way to get buy-in from the students is to ask them what members of the group can do to make the experience a success for everyone and what actions should be out of bounds. Brainstorm everything they can think of, writing it on a chalkboard or big piece of paper as they think out loud. Then ask them to work together to rank the positive behaviors in order of importance; you may need to fill in if there are any really important things they have forgotten. If a student is out of line —

especially if she is insulting or silencing another student — you should immediately make it clear that such behavior cannot be tolerated. You may only have to do this once if you do it firmly and clearly the first time.

Managing behavior doesn't have to be negative very often. The more you reinforce positive behaviors, the more of them you'll see. Try saying, "Sally, I know you have an opinion you're dying to get out, but you didn't interrupt Xiao and I really appreciate that. Now, tell us what you think!" Sally will keep participating without interrupting, and other members of the group will see the learning value and group harmony created by behaving considerately.

SUCCESS STORY:

STUDENT-RUN GROUPS

WITHOUT FAIL, ERIN ALWAYS GETS A COLD MID-WAY THROUGH THE SEMESTER. BECAUSE SHE WAS RUNNING GROUPS OF COLLEGE STUDENTS, THEY DIDN'T REQUIRE ADULT SUPERVISION, SO SHE TAUGHT HER STUDENTS TO RUN THEIR OWN GROUPS IF SHE HAD TO BE ABSENT. YOU CAN USE THE SAME TECHNIQUES TO SUPPORT STUDENTS WHO WANT TO SET UP THEIR OWN STUDY GROUPS.

IT'S HELPFUL TO HAVE SOME FORM OF FACILITATION IN PLACE SO THAT STUDENTS DON'T DISTRACT EACH OTHER. ERIN TOLD HER STUDENTS THAT IF SHE HAD TO MISS A GROUP, THEY SHOULD COME TO THE USUAL ROOM, CHOOSE A FACILITATOR TO PUT THE AGENDA ON THE BOARD AND KEEP THE GROUP ON TRACK, AND CONDUCT BUSINESS AS USUAL. THE NEXT TIME SHE GOT SICK, THAT'S WHAT THEY DID.

IF YOU ARE RUNNING STUDENT-CENTERED GROUPS, THE PARTICIPANTS ARE ALREADY SOMEWHAT IN CONTROL OF THEIR LEARNING, SO POINT OUT TO THEM HOW MUCH THEY ALREADY KNOW ABOUT WHAT AND HOW THEY WANT TO STUDY. GIVE EACH STUDENT OPPORTUNITIES TO TAKE CHARGE — FOR EXAMPLE, IF YOU USE A SIGN-IN SHEET, HAVE A DIFFERENT STUDENT RETURN IT TO YOU DURING EACH SESSION. EXPLAIN TO YOUR STUDENTS THAT THE ACT OF TALKING THROUGH PROBLEMS OR QUESTIONS WITH EACH OTHER IS USEFUL, WHETHER OR NOT THEY KNOW ALL THE ANSWERS. DISCUSSIONS PROVIDE AN OPPORTUNITY TO THINK DEEPLY ABOUT THE TOPIC AT HAND, WHICH HELPS STUDENTS RETAIN INFORMATION, AND PROVIDE NEW PERSPECTIVES, TOO. WITH THE RIGHT PREPARATION, THE ABSENCE OF A TUTOR CAN BE A GREAT WAY FOR STUDENTS TO DISCOVER JUST HOW GOOD THEIR FACILITATION AND LEADERSHIP SKILLS ARE. (AND REMEMBER, THIS ONLY WORKS FOR STUDENTS AGES 18 AND OLDER — NEVER LEAVE CHILDREN UNDER YOUR CARE ALONE!)

Group Facilitation and Time Management

In one of her first group tutoring sessions, Erin had a student who loved to talk. (There's usually at least one.) As she sat listening to him drone on, she thought, ""Someone needs to tell this guy to wrap it up." Then she realized that someone was her. When you're the group facilitator, that someone is you. Keep a close eye on time and make sure the group is meeting its goals. If the students started the session with the intention to practice writing short stories but are now recounting Stephen King plots to one another, you should get everyone back to the short stories. Don't keep students past the scheduled session — everyone is busy, and kids will most likely have parents waiting in the parking lot for them. The group tutoring train can quickly derail without the leader's sharp time management skills.

A good facilitator keeps the conversation flowing and on topic without dominating it. The purpose of facilitating a tutoring group is not to tell the students what you know about the subject or share your opinions, as tempting as both can be. Your job is to help the students exchange ideas and to step in when the process breaks down. Ask open-ended questions and let the students answer them fully. If a student asks for help, see if another student can provide some suggestions first, but tactfully correct any misinformation. When it's time to move on to a new topic, lead the way. All you have to say is, "Okay, everyone, that's all the time we've got for sine, tangent, and cosine this time. What's next on the agenda?" The students will follow, and they'll be grateful to you for helping them cover all the topics they need to study.

Success Story: Hushing Henry

Henry was a rambler. He loved to make group discussions about himself as much as possible — his experiences in class, what he wanted for lunch, the recent operation on his arm, and on and on. Worse, his social skills were weak, so he didn't pick up on Erin's efforts to steer the conversation way from him. She'd interrupt by saying, "Thanks, Henry. Brittany, what do you think?" but he'd keep talking, oblivious.

Erin was well within her rights to ask him to stop attending the group, but she decided to try to help him instead. After the next session, Erin asked Henry to stay afterwards with her. His behavior was so irritating that it was difficult to praise him honestly, but she began by saying she appreciated his interest in the groups and his regular attendance. Then she told him his behavior was causing problems for her and the other students. "I do want you to talk sometimes, but you need to talk about what

THE GROUP IS DISCUSSING AND GIVE OTHER PEOPLE A CHANCE TO SPEAK, TOO." HENRY APOLOGIZED AND SAID HE WOULD DO BETTER. MUCH TO ERIN'S SURPRISE, HE NEVER CAUSED PROBLEMS DURING HIS GROUP AGAIN. EVEN THOUGH IT CAN BE SCARY TO FACE A POSSIBLE CONFLICT, TELLING STUDENTS HOW TO BEHAVE APPROPRIATELY CAN BE THE BEST WAY TO CHANGE THEIR BEHAVIOR FOR THE BETTER.

Get Everyone Involved

One of the biggest challenges of running a group is getting appropriate levels of involvement from every member. There are always some students who are more comfortable speaking out than others. Teachers in some countries don't encourage students to reflect out loud or ask questions, so if your students have been to school elsewhere you may need to explain that participating in the discussion is expected. Other students are simply shy, sometimes as a result of bad experiences with teachers or fellow students. Don't hesitate to talk to your students about these differences and tell them that you want everyone to participate equally in the group. Then give them some tools to make that happen.

One way to start the conversation is to have the students reflect, either out loud or in writing, about how they tend to act in groups. If they're having trouble, toss out some adjectives and ask them to write down the ones that apply to them: shy, chatty, sociable, serious, giggly, quiet, thoughtful, scared, talkative, nervous. Then challenge the very talkative students to make room for the quiet ones to speak and encourage the quiet students to speak when they have something to say.

If you've got a lot of students who aren't contributing to the conversation, try having them write before talking. Instead of asking them to talk about the important events of World War I, for instance, have them spend five to ten minutes jotting down their ideas first. Let them refer to their notes or books. Then when you start the discussion, everyone will have something to say.

Other times, you may have too many students fighting for the floor, and they may interrupt each other. You can solve that problem by bringing a talking stick (or any other object) and announcing that whoever is speaking must be holding the talking stick. If a student is not holding the talking stick, he should be listening to the person who is. You can also limit the amount of time a person can have the stick — say, students can talk for three minutes before they have to pass the stick to someone else. Not only will this help the discussions flow more smoothly, it's also fun.

Top 7 Tips: Group Tutoring and Workshops

1. When you're running a group, position yourself as a trustworthy ally. Show the students that you're there to support them while maintaining group structure.

2. Prepare for ongoing tutoring group sessions by familiarizing yourself with the material the students are covering and developing a repertoire of activities you can adapt to different topics.

3. Keep your time management skills keenly honed, and redirect the group if the discussion veers away from the topic.

4. Ask the students to set behavioral expectations for the group, then make sure the members of the group (including you!) live up to them.

5. Give students as many opportunities as possible to take charge of their learning.

6. Build trust within the group by pointing out students' academic strengths and explaining how different abilities can be complementary.

7. Find interesting ways to get everyone in the group participating about the same amount, such as using a talking stick or having students reflect on their participation styles.

Be a Great Tutor

Chapter 9: The Interpersonal Side of Learning and Tutoring

Falling in Like

Everyone wants to be liked, and your students are no exception. Because so much of successful tutoring depending on a positive relationship between tutor and student, you must find something to like about every student you work with. Just the feeling of rejection can affect student performance negatively. Likewise, trusting that a tutor or teacher cares about him and wants him to succeed can change a fearful, reluctant student into a motivated, engaged one.

We know this is sometimes easier said than done. You'll find students you adore — they remind you of yourself at their age, maybe, or they have good social skills that make them easy to be around. In other cases, you'll have to dig to find the connection. Remember, students act out their anxieties. Some students are terrified of teachers (and, by extension, you), so it may take several sessions before a scared student begins to relax. Others may be very defensive and want to talk over you.

When student behaviors bother you, think about why the student is behaving the way he is and what you could do to change the situation. If you have a restless 10-year-old in your office, for example, resist the temptation to load her up with more work that will keep her quiet. Instead, ask her to do jumping jacks for five minutes and then continue your work. She'll be much easier to tutor, and much easier to like.

If you can't find a way to like your student, you'll have to refer her to someone else. The student can sense your dislike, even if you think you're concealing it, and that turns tutoring into a damaging experience for her. See "Making a Graceful Exit" later in this chapter for advice on how to end a tutoring relationship.

Connecting the Dots: Working with Everyone Else in the Student's Life

When you become a tutor, you sign on to work with more people than just the student, especially when you are working with children and teens. Their parents will almost always be involved in setting the tutoring agenda — in fact, the parents may be much more enthusiastic about tutoring than the student is. Some children have other caretakers, too, such as nannies or grandparents, and you may need to coordinate scheduling or payment with them. Obviously, social skills are crucial to your success as a tutor.

Make sure you know who is in charge, and deal directly

with that person. If there are several caretakers involved, ask for a "point person" with whom to arrange logistics. As you work regularly with a student, try to communicate only with that person. Don't ask others, especially the student, to deliver information to the point person for you, as that will send mixed messages. Mentioning a scheduling problem to a fourth-grader will only put her in the middle.

Good Fences Make Good Tutors

You can prevent potential problems by setting clear boundaries and expectations at the beginning of your tutoring relationship. Erin once found herself in a tricky situation that she could have headed off with better communication at the beginning. She tutored a child in the afternoons, when his nanny was usually his caretaker, but his parents were often in and out, too. When Erin's tutoring session was over, it often took the nanny and parents five to ten minutes to coordinate her payment, with the nanny yelling upstairs to the mother to ask if she had money in her purse. The situation was time-consuming and a little embarrassing for Erin, who would have much preferred a monthly check mailed to her house, but she couldn't think of a way to address the situation without more awkwardness than it was worth. If she'd said up front what she wanted, though, she could have gotten it without any discomfort at all. Lesson learned? Think about exactly what you want from your tutoring relationships and put it all on the table up front.

Many families try to push your time boundaries, arriving late or canceling at the last minute and asking you to make up the time. We recommend you hold the line as much as possible. If a student is 15 minutes to your session, end when you normally would and charge your usual fee, even though the session is shorter than it was supposed to be. Their lateness isn't your fault, and you shouldn't be penalized for it, even if you were just going home aftewards. Similarly, we recommend that you charge your full fee if students cancel with less than 24 hours' notice. Your clients will respect you as a professional, and they'll think twice before canceling on you again. If your clients experience a true emergency, such as a death in the family, you can always waive your cancellation fee.

You may not be able to anticipate every issue that arises. You're only human, and families can be full of surprises. If it's important to you to make a change, you'll need to say so pleasantly and straightforwardly to whoever's in charge.

Making a Graceful Exit

Not every tutoring relationship is a good fit. Erin once worked with a student she liked very much whose parents were so critical and demanding of her as a tutor that she couldn't continue tutoring their daughter, Emily. They were critical and demanding of Emily, too, and Erin was tempted to stay in hopes of being a reasonable, positive adult influence in the girl's life. Ultimately, though, working with that family took too much of a toll on Erin. In some situations, you may be able to offer a referral, but in this case Erin wasn't willing to recommend any of her colleagues. She did give advance notice, though, and let Emily know how much she'd enjoyed their time together.

Leaving a tutoring relationship can certainly be awkward. Think about how you can leave with your integrity intact, and remember that you don't need to explain your decision unless you want to and feel it would be productive. Be careful about lying, though — if you claim you can't tutor on Tuesdays and then begin working with a child up the street that day, the folks you lied to may find out. Remember, you are free to leave, just as your clients are always free to end the tutoring relationship with you. If you can, it's best to end on a positive note, since your success as an independent tutor is built on a good reputation among families. (See Chapter 11 for information on working successfully as an independent tutor.)

Don't Get Caught Up in Someone Else's Divorce

Many divorced parents have civil relationships with each other. That said, if you work with children, you'll find that a lot of divorced parents are barely speaking, much less communicating effectively with each other about their child's education. The kids, and sometimes the tutor, can get caught in a painful power play. Don't let the parents use you as a go-between to share information about their child's schooling, and don't undertake something unusual, such as a field trip, to which both parents haven't consented.

Make sure everyone agrees on what your sessions should cover. For instance, you may have one parent who wants you to focus on math and another who thinks the sessions should center on English skills. They need to decide and give you a unified message before you can proceed. Insist on it before you start — otherwise, these waters can rise quickly.

Tutoring Diverse Populations

Diversity takes many forms. Although we tend to associate the term with racial and ethnic diversity, it can refer to all sorts of differences. Your students may come from a variety of family structures, including those with two moms or two dads; various class backgrounds; public, private, or parochial schools; and different grades. They may have a variety of learning styles and strengths.

It's a good idea to root out some of the assumptions you might be making about your students ahead of time. For example, many people unconsciously assume that working-class students will eventually take working-class jobs, so a tutor might be more apt to mention carpentry as a future career than architecture. Help your students expand their possibilities by encouraging them to think of the most interesting, creative, and rewarding ways they might use their skills.

We all make assumptions based on gender, race, age, and other factors, and we must be vigilant in countering those biases. When you meet a student for the first time, notice what assumptions you make: for example, if she is a young mother, do you assume she wants a job that allows her to spend a lot of time at home? She may or may not. Students may also make assumptions about their own potential based on their gender, race, age, or other factor, so you should keep an eye on both their biases and your own.

The only way to find out whether your assumptions are true or not is to get to know your student. Find out what she wants, help her work toward that, and encourage her to expand her vision.

Recognizing Child Abuse

We heartily hope you'll never encounter child abuse in your tutoring, but it's possible you will. Furthermore, a tutor may see signs of abuse before any other adult in the child's life, and students are likely to confide in a tutor they've come to know and trust. If a child tells you she is being physically or sexually abused, believe her and act accordingly. Ignoring abuse only perpetuates it. According to www.childwelfare.gov, the following signs may signal the presence of child abuse or neglect:

The Child:

- Shows sudden changes in behavior or school performance
- Has not received help for physical or medical problems brought to the parents' attention
- Has learning problems (or difficulty concentrating) that cannot be attributed to specific physical or psychological causes
- Is always watchful, as though preparing for something bad to happen
- Lacks adult supervision
- Is overly compliant, passive, or withdrawn
- Comes to school or other activities early, stays late, and does not want to go home

The Parent:

- Shows little concern for the child
- Denies the existence of — or blames the child for — the child's problems in school or at home
- Asks teachers or other caregivers to use harsh physical discipline if the child misbehaves
- Sees the child as entirely bad, worthless, or burdensome
- Demands a level of physical or academic performance the child cannot achieve
- Looks primarily to the child for care, attention, and satisfaction of emotional needs

The Parent and Child:

- Rarely touch or look at each other
- Consider their relationship entirely negative
- State that they do not like each other

If you see signs of child abuse, you must report it to your local Child Protective Services. Not only do you have a moral responsibility to the child, you also have a legal one. To report possible child abuse in the United States, call 800-4-A-Child or visit http://www.childwelfare.gov/responding/reporting.cfm.

Top 5 Tips: The Interpersonal Side of Learning and Tutoring

1. Find a way to make a personal connection with each student and find something you like about him or her.

2. Identify a "point person" early in your tutoring relationship and always communicate directly with that person.

3. Never put a child in the middle of your communications with the child's parents or caregivers.

4. If you need to end a tutoring relationship, try to exit gracefully. Don't like, but don't ruin your reputation if you can help it.

5. Continually notice and challenge your own biases and expectations.

Be a Great Tutor

Chapter 10: E-tutoring

Online — or "e-tutoring" — is a rapidly growing option for students and tutors alike. E-tutoring may be a useful part of your repertoire as a tutor, or you may choose to focus on e-tutoring exclusively, especially if you are in an area where in-person tutoring is difficult. According to Prashant Yadav, CEO of Etutelage.com, one of the main advantages for both e-tutors and e-tutorees is that no one has to travel. So if you dream of earning a living from home, or just want to help out a friend studying far away, e-tutoring skills can be a great resource. What does it take to succeed as an e-tutor? All your in-person tutoring skills, plus a bit of tech savvy, extra flexibility, and the ability to make a personal connection online.

Tech Tips for E-Tutoring

You don't have to be a computer genius to e-tutor, but you'll want a basic level of comfort with email, programs such as Microsoft Office, Skype, and, of course, the Internet. Obviously, you'll also want to be well-trained in whatever software you're using for e-tutoring and to know enough about computers that you don't melt down during a routine software update.

If you're just starting out e-tutoring, your first task is to learn the software you're using thoroughly. You need to know how to use it, of course, but you also need to be able to help students when they get stuck. If you work for a company, they will provide you with software and a computer connection, of course. If you are tutoring online independently, Skype or a similar service works well. Many institutions provide online "classrooms" and other online tutoring resources, so check with your administrator if you are tutoring at a school.

When working with a student who is new to e-tutoring, set aside some time at the beginning of your first few sessions to allow your student to get familiar with the software program; remember, there will inevitably be some glitches and confusion in any new task, so be patient with the process. Bear in mind that your student is learning a valuable new skill by navigating this online process with you. You may be using software that includes an audio component, which will allow you to talk your student through any technological stumbling blocks, or you may not have audio available. In the latter case, the "chat" component is the main way you'll communicate with your student. We recommend using audio if possible.

Brush up on your computer vocabulary. For example: What's that key with the squiggly mark in the upper left-hand side of your keyboard? It's called a tilda. Kids, especially, are often quite computer-literate, so even if your friends don't know what you mean, most likely they will — and they may have a lot to teach you. Knowing terms saves you time and trouble.

Making a Personal Connection Online

Students' attention can wander in nearly any tutoring session, but the lack of person-to-person contact makes it especially easy for students to get distracted or lose interest during an e-tutoring session, says Yadav. "We encourage our teachers to continuously keep checking with the student if he is really following and keep asking leading questions to verify that in real time." If your student doesn't respond to you, don't assume she's working extra math problems. She may be texting her friends about a party next weekend, talking to someone else in the room, or simply daydreaming through her session. Having video helps, but doesn't eliminate, the difficulty.

Whatever your technological set-up, you'll need to make an extra effort to create a personal connection with your student. Eye contact and body language are two of the main ways people communicate respect, caring, and interest — all crucial to a successful tutoring relationship. You'll want to pay special attention to the tone of your voice and/or online chat with the student to make sure you convey appropriate friendliness and professionalism.

Example: Hi Mika. I know you have a test tomorrow, so let's get started.

Analysis: Delivered in person, these two sentences could sound warm, engaged, and caring with the right body language and tone of voice. But online they could come across as stiff, bossy, and impatient, depending on the reader's interpretation.

Revised example: Hi Mika! :-) I hope you're not too stressed about that test tomorrow. Do you want to check in first or get started now?

Analysis: Caring and interest come across more clearly here, with the exclamation point, "emoticon" (a combination of symbols that creates a "facial" expression on the computer), a statement expressing hope for the student's well-being, and a question about how she wants to proceed.

Stay Flexible

All tutors need to be flexible, but e-tutors will have to adjust to changing circumstances more than most — for one thing, your sessions may be back-to-back, without the usual down-time as you travel between students or take a quick coffee break between appointments. E-tutoring software changes all the time; most of the change are improvements, but they can still be nerveracking. Moreover, best practices in e-tutoring are being developed, so new methods and strategies will be continually implemented in the coming years. That's part of what makes e-tutoring exciting: it's a wide-open new field. That's also what requires extra flexibility and its indispensable sidekick, patience.

Advantages to E-Tutoring

Although e-tutoring has some drawbacks, it also has some compensating advantages for the student and tutor. For example, most programs allow the tutor to easily post any computer document to the tutoring "room." When appropriate, you will likely be able to navigate to relevant web pages with your student. When doing group tutoring online, one student can post, say, a difficult math problem and the others can work together to solve it. Furthermore, shy students are sometimes able to be more active and outgoing online than they are in person, so working with a student online may open up new lines of communication.

Top 5 Tips: E-Tutoring

1. Know your software so that your tutoring sessions aren't interrupted with (your) technical difficulties.

2. Early in your tutoring, set aside time for your student to learn how to use the software, too.

3. Continually check in during your online session to be sure the student remains connected.

4. Be aware of "tone" in online exchanges, and make sure to keep yours warm yet professional.

5. Stay flexible and be patient as this field evolves. Online tutoring is growing in popularity and changes to protocol are ongoing.

Chapter 11: How to Be an Independent Tutor

You don't need to earn a living from tutoring to call yourself a tutor — just think of all the parents, classroom teachers, peer tutors and others who are tutoring — but many people do earn part or all of their income from independent tutoring. Many others work for a tutoring agency and act semi-independently, receiving students from the agency and sharing their hourly wage with the agency as well. Erin and Chris each built their own independent tutoring practice, finding students and maintaining relationships with schools and other referral sources. If you're interested in going that route, this chapter is for you: how to make tutoring your livelihood.

Step 1: Is Tutoring the Right Business For Me?

Working as an independent tutor has its perks: you can establish your own schedule, you receive all of the hourly tutoring rate, and often, that rate compares favorably with other part-time work you might find. In some major United States cities, rates for well-known tutors can be very high, on a par with hourly fees charged by lawyers, accountants and other skilled hourly professionals. Of course, it all depends on presenting yourself well, talking to the right people, and building a stable base of students.

Pro's & Con's of the Tutoring Business

Pro	Con
Flexible scheduling: You decide when to work and which days to take off. Taking the summer off or a monthlong vacation in December for overseas travel? Tutoring is a great job in between.	You have to manage and pay for all the things a business would cover for you: In the US, that means health plans, taxes, retirement benefits, business insurance, and savings to cover sick days and vacations
High hourly rate. Depending on your skills, perhaps very high ($100+ per hour for expert tutors in urban U.S. areas)	Sessions tend to be on evenings and weekends, making you busy when your friends and family are likely to be free
Satisfaction of teaching one-on-one and seeing your students overcome challenges. When you've spent a day tutoring, you can rest easy knowing you've done some good in the world.	It can take some time to build a stable base of students; in the meantime your earnings may be lower than desired.
Compatibility with other work or life responsibilities (for example, with being a parent). By the way, your child's school is a great place to start looking for tutoring clients.	Income will wax and wane depending on the time of year and number of students you have at any given time.
The opportunity to use academic skills outside academia.	You may need to provide your own transportation among students' homes

Step 2: Who, What, When, Where?

So you've decided to become an independent tutor —
congratulations! Your next step is to gather the basic information
that will help you decide where to focus and how to present
yourself. First, we need to get some details:

What ages of students do you have experience in working
with, and what ages do you think you'll be able to work with
successfully? Be sure to define this specifically — if you tell
someone that you can teach all ages, they may be skeptical unless
you've had that specific experience.

What subjects are you able to tutor? Don't forget areas
such as organizational help and study skills, which are often in
high demand.

Where will the tutoring take place? Many tutors travel to
students' homes, but others meet in libraries or schools. Erin and
Chris have done a little of each, but found that parents strongly
prefer tutors who can travel to the home in the after-school,
evening or weekend hours. If so, how far are you willing to
travel? Most tutors do not charge for their transportation time, so
this could be a significant factor.

When are you available to tutor? Can you commit to being
available at that same time every week for most of the semester
or school year?

As you gather that information, consider writing it up into

a Basic Service Sheet; a customizable sample is available for your use in the online Resource Guide. Now there is just one other big question: how much will you charge? To answer that, a little investigation is required:

If you have any friends who are tutors, ask them for their rates. How did they come up with that number? What experience, age focus or subject expertise do they have?

Figure out where other tutors in your community advertise, and see what rates they suggest — as we'll discuss later, that could mean parents groups, schools, websites and online community "bulletin boards," or local newspapers. Try to gather an informal survey of typical rates based on these sources.

Ask a few parents or teachers you know what they would suggest as a typical rate; if they're not sure, try a few numbers on them. Don't sell yourself short! In many areas, tutors are in high demand, and people are often willing to pay a significant amount for your one-on-one help.

Think through your qualifications. If you have, say, a master's degree in Chemistry, you can charge more for science tutoring than someone who doesn't. If you don't have an advanced degree in a subject, but you did well in it in school and can convincingly demonstrate expertise, you may be able to charge almost as much as someone who does have the degree.

Demand for special skills is a factor, too. Highly qualified math and science tutors are often in great demand, as are tutors who specialize in standardized test and college entrance preparation. There are specific niches where many people may want skilled tutors and be willing to pay for them — for example, English as a Second Language tutoring may be in great demand among the families of foreign diplomats or business people.

Parents or adult students may ask you if your rate changes for longer sessions, or if there are two or more students involved in the session. Include this in your informal survey, and see how other tutors in the area address this. Chris and Erin offer a small discount for longer sessions (90 minutes), because they feel this offers the chance for more effective tutoring with each student, and also reduces their transportation time. For additional students, they charge an additional hourly fee of about 25% more per student because of the extra preparation needed.

Bear in mind that your rate covers more than just the hour you spend with the student. Calculate all your time and expenses, and make sure your fee covers them. Talking to parents and teachers, preparing for lessons, and getting from one student's house to the next can take up a lot of time, so remember that your hourly fee covers all those parts of tutoring. Also, keep in mind that your hourly rate has to make up for those days when students are sick, or on vacation, or when you're on vacation, so even if it seems like you would earn a lot during a full week of tutoring, remember that you have to store some of your hourly earnings for those rainy days. And don't forget: you'll have to pay taxes, too.

You might want to offer different rates depending on the location. You could charge one hourly fee for student who comes to you and an additional fee for your travel time if you go to them. If you charge for travel, don't base the fee on mileage — rush hour traffic, which is when you're likely to be traveling between students, can make time much more significant than miles travelled.

For help calculating all these variables, visit www.tutoring-expert.com/tutoring-rates.html for up-to-date information on the range of tutoring rates.

TUTORING FOR SOCIAL JUSTICE

MOST INDEPENDENT TUTORS WORK FOR FAMILIES WHO CAN PAY THEM, OF COURSE — OTHERWISE THEY MIGHT NOT BE INDEPENDENT TUTORS FOR VERY LONG! BUT THERE ARE MANY FAMILIES WHOSE CHILDREN COULD BENEFIT HUGELY FROM TUTORING, AND ADULTS WHO NEED HELP GETTING THROUGH SCHOOL, WHO CANNOT AFFORD TO HIRE AN INDEPENDENT TUTOR. SOME OF THEM ARE ABLE TO ACCESS FREE OR LOW-COST TUTORING SERVICES THROUGH LOCAL SCHOOLS OR NON-PROFITS, BUT SADLY, MOST DO NOT GET THE HELP THEY NEED. IF YOU ARE INTERESTED IN HELPING AS A VOLUNTEER TUTOR, IT CAN BE SOME OF THE MOST SATISFYING WORK YOU DO, AND CAN BE COMBINED WITH YOUR PAID TUTORING WORK. FOR EXAMPLE, SOME

TUTORS DECIDE THAT FOR EVERY FIVE PAYING STUDENTS, THEY WILL WORK WITH ONE FOR FREE; OTHERS TAKE ON ONE FREE STUDENT AT A TIME, REGARDLESS OF HOW MANY OTHER STUDENTS THEY WORK WITH. YOU MIGHT ALSO CONSIDER OFFERING A LOW-FEE TIME SLOT. WHEN YOU AGREE TO DO FREE OR LOW-COST TUTORING, MENTION YOUR REGULAR FEE, TOO. KNOWING HOW MUCH YOUR FREE OR LOW-COST SERVICE IS WORTH TO OTHERS CAN BE A POWERFUL MOTIVATOR FOR YOUR STUDENT.

IF YOU'RE INTERESTED, A LOCAL LIBRARY, NON-PROFIT OR PUBLIC SCHOOL CAN PROBABLY DIRECT YOU TOWARD A PROGRAM OR STUDENT WHO NEEDS YOUR HELP. ALL FAMILIES, PAYING OR NOT, WILL APPRECIATE YOUR EFFORTS TO HELP THEIR CHILDREN, BUT INCLUDING SOME VOLUNTEER TUTORING CAN BE A WONDERFUL EXPERIENCE.

Step 3: How do I present myself?

You probably hear all the time about the importance of presenting yourself in a "professional" way, but what exactly does that mean? In your materials, it means well-written, well-designed documents that show people you've thought carefully about how your tutoring service will function and have anticipated their most common questions. We'll help you create these in a moment.

In person, being "professional" as a tutor means showing

that you are friendly, focused, and skilled in your subject area, able to answer questions directly and calmly, and confident in your abilities. You don't need to wear a suit for tutoring, but you should look neat and well-groomed. Highly fashionable or revealing clothes will only be a distraction, so save those for Saturday night. And, of course, arrive on time with your cell phone turned off.

Let's start with the minimum materials you'll need (all of which are available in customizable format in the online Resource Guide):

1) A well-written résumé describing your academic background, education-related experience, and some academic accomplishments or areas of strength.

2) A business card with your name and relevant contact information, and perhaps your specialties as a tutor. These can often be printed very cheaply through online services.

3) A Reference Document, listing at least three references, each of whom have agreed to act as a reference for you. Write a sentence describing the context in which you've known the reference (for example, "John was my supervisor at O'Briant Test Prep, where we worked together to prepare students for college entrance exams"), and include their contact information, preferably a phone number. Ideally at least two of these references will be in an education-related field, but if not they can be "character references" or references from other

employers.

4) Basic Information Sheet: As described above, this includes your rates, how far you will travel and when you are willing to be available, and your areas of focus or expertise. Remember that saying you cover all subjects in all ages is unlikely, and parents will recognize that. You might say something like: "Focus on math and science-related areas, with experience working with grades 6-12."

5) Sample Contract: This describes what you offer and what your expectations are, in terms of rates, prompt payment, advance notice of cancellations, coverage of extra costs for books and other materials, etc. The Resource Guide offers a good example of a tutoring contract.

PRESENTING YOURSELF ONLINE: YOUR FREE YEARLONG RESOURCE FROM TUTORING-EXPERT.COM

AN EXCELLENT AND INCREASINGLY IMPORTANT WAY TO PRESENT YOURSELF, AND TO IMPRESS YOUR POTENTIAL CLIENTS, IS TO CREATE AN ONLINE PROFESSIONAL TUTORING PROFILE. THIS CAN BE AS SIMPLE AS A SITE WITH YOUR NAME, PERHAPS A PHOTOGRAPH, AND A SUMMARY OF YOUR QUALIFICATIONS, LOCATION, AND AREAS OF SPECIALTY. MAKE SURE YOUR PROFILE LISTS YOUR CONTACT INFORMATION, INCLUDING AN EMAIL ADDRESS THAT YOU CHECK REGULARLY.

OWNERS OF THIS BOOK ARE INVITED TO POST A PROFILE ON WWW.TUTORING-EXPERT.COM FOR FREE (A $20 VALUE) FOR ONE YEAR. YOU'LL BENEFIT FROM THE STEADILY INCREASING TRAFFIC ON THE SITE AND POLISH YOUR CREDENTIALS AS A TUTOR. AFTER ALL, YOU GET TO BE ONE OF THE TUTORING EXPERTS.

POST AT WWW.TUTORING-EXPERT.COM/PROFILE.HTML.

(PASSWORD TUTORINGSUCCESS).

Step 4: Finding Clients & Spreading the Word

So you've identified your focus areas and developed the materials to present yourself well — now it's time to find your students! Here is a simple process that has worked well for Chris, Erin, and thousands of other tutors:

Start with your friends and family. They know and trust you, and may be able to refer you to their own networks of friends. Make sure to provide them with a supply of your business cards to share with friends, and ask them to let you know whenever a friend indicates interest. It's worth calling that person to follow up and see if they are interested, as soon as you hear about it. When you ask anyone for advice, whether they have any or not, make sure to ask them if there is anyone they recommend speaking with for more advice or referrals. Sooner or later, you'll find someone who can be of great help.

Introduce yourself to the people who are with students every day: guidance counselors, learning specialists, teachers, school administrators, youth program leaders, babysitters, speech therapists, etc. If you know any people personally who are in these professions, begin with them. Otherwise, try calling local schools, public and private. Describe briefly that you are a private tutor, and ask if you could drop by to introduce yourself and leave some materials. At most schools, especially if you can get through to a counselor or learning specialist, dropping off your materials is not too much to ask. Some may never call you, but if you can meet someone there and make even a small personal connection, you never know when they may refer a student to you. If you do make a personal contact, be sure to send them a thank-you note for their time, and follow-up with them after three to four weeks to see if any students have come along who might benefit from your tutoring. If you're interested in tutoring college and graduate school students, call local colleges and universities and ask if you may post flyers on campus; many will allow it. Almost every college has tutoring programs, so find the faculty member in charge of those programs and ask if you could drop off your materials to him or her. Especially at public schools, the tutoring programs tend to be in great demand and may welcome a person willing to take their referrals.

Post information about yourself on bulletin boards (for example at the library, local coffeeshops, schools, etc), with parent groups (online or in-person groups), with online bulletin boards, and at any other place in your community where you can imagine parents, teachers or students might look for help. You may want to consider placing a small paid notice in the newspaper or other local publication.

Look for tutor referral networks or companies; in some cities there are agencies that match students to tutors for a fee, or that take a portion of the family's payment and pay you the rest for any students they match with you. Try an online search to see if any such companies are in your area. While they may not provide as much income for you, they can be a great way to get started and begin building your experience and contacts.

With all of these techniques, your patience and dedication will make all the difference. Don't count on any one contact to produce referrals — make sure you speak with many people about your services, post information everywhere you can think of, and speak with many local schools. Perhaps only 1 in 10 will provide a referral, but each referral could turn into a family you work with for years, or better yet, a family that begins to refer their friends to you. As Chris and Erin found, once you have stable, positive relationships with a few families, they will begin suggesting your name to friends, and after some time you may even have a waiting list for your services! Just remember that it can take months to build your initial base of students. Be patient and make sure to have a financial backup plan in case the startup process goes a little slower than you anticipate. But with perseverance, you will eventually find the right contacts.

Talking to a Potential Client

Once you receive a referral or are contacted by an interested parent, they may want to get to know you better before committing to hiring you. Offer to stop by their home for a 30-minute introductory session, during which time you can talk with the parents and with the student. Use this time as an opportunity to get to know them and offer some initial suggestions about what you could do to help. Parents will appreciate your honesty, and even if you say that you are not an expert in all the areas needed by the child, they may appreciate your honesty so much that they'll bring you in to help in those areas you know best. Of course, make sure to highlight your experience and any specific techniques you would suggest, such as those mentioned in the earlier chapters in this book, so that parents have faith in your abilities.

Step 5. Acing Your First Session

When you arrive at your first session, plan to take the lead in a friendly way. Start by asking everyone involved about their goals for tutoring, listening carefully, and coming up with a set of realistic goals together (if your student is a child, be sure to listen to her, not just her parents). Review the main areas of focus that the parent and child believe are needed, making sure you have a written record of them in your notes. Make sure that their expectations are realistic: if their child is struggling with a particular subject, for example, explain that there is unlikely to be a "quick fix." Instead, thoughtful one-on-one work will allow you and your student to gradually understand the student's strengths and challenges and address areas of difficulty.

When you first begin a new tutoring relationship, it will both save you time and demonstrate your professionalism if you discuss several important details up front. Walk the parents through your contract, explaining the various policies, the rates, and your expectations around payment. Be clear about how and when you want to receive payment and what you expect to be compensated for (for example, if you talk with a teacher for 15 minutes or fewer, you might not charge extra, but for longer conversations you might charge a portion of your hourly fee). Explain your cancellation policy; Erin and Chris both require full payment if a student cancels with less than 24 hours' notice.

Many people are happy to pay you monthly so that you don't have to collect fees at every session. Don't be embarrassed to talk about money — after all, this is a business arrangement. Ask them to sign two copies of the contract, which you can then sign as well: one for their records and one for yours.

After that, discuss a schedule and, if possible, map out the next several sessions. Ask how long the parents (or adult students) think they will want your services and whether they are planning any major breaks in tutoring, perhaps when school isn't in session. Everyone will rest easy knowing that you've thought this process through and have established a basic plan.

After that first session, create a document outlining your expectations. If you're working with a young child, it's often helpful to make a big chart he can color in as he reaches his goals. For adults, a simple checklist or spreadsheet might be best. Use this document regularly to track your student's progress.

Step 6: Maintaining a Successful Tutoring Practice

Good Communication: Working with Children

Beyond your relationship and assistance to the student herself, the most important factor in your success is good communication. First, that means good communication with the parents:

- Make sure they always know what you're working on with their child.

- Mentions strengths you see in their child as well as areas of struggle.

- Describe how you are addressing the student's "challenge areas." Include any ideas you have as to why those areas have been difficult for the student (as we describe earlier, students themselves often have the best insight into this, if you listen carefully).

- Describe the realistic goals and progress you expect to see.

- As a best practice, we recommend requiring an adult (other than you) to be present at all times; this protects you from liability. They don't need to sit in on the tutoring session, and in fact that is usually not recommended; but an adult (parent or otherwise) should be in the home or building at all times during your session.

This also means good communication with the student's school, especially if someone at the school provided the initial referral. If the parents give you the green light, you may want to set aside some time to visit or call one of your student's teachers, particularly in an area where the student has had difficulty.

(Remember, though, that your student and her parents trust your discretion, so don't share any sensitive information unless you've cleared it with the family. Also, bear in mind that some parents will not want you to talk to their child's teachers, even for free.) Teachers are almost always relieved to know that a professional tutor is working with one of their students. Ask the teacher if they have any observations or suggestions that might help your tutoring. These can be extremely useful, since the teacher has likely spent significant time with the student. Showing the parents that you have heard and are working with these suggestions will impress them as well. If you're able to establish a connection with one of the student's teachers, counselors, learning specialists or school administrators, make sure to check in with them from time to time, providing an update and asking for suggestions or any changes they've seen in your student.

Good Communication: Working with Adults

No matter who is paying for your tutoring services, if your student is over age 18, you need his permission to discuss his progress with anyone else, including his parents or spouse. Adult students are usually ready and able to talk about their needs and progress with you themselves; having family members out of the picture can leave you with more time to work directly with the student. Although some may want you to talk with their professors, others may be horrified at the very idea, so don't assume direct communication with adult students' teachers is welcome. Many prefer not to let anyone know they need tutoring at all.

You'll still need to set reasonable goals with adult students and give them regular feedback on their progress, focusing on both strengths and areas of difficulty. Adults may have even more insight than children about their own abilities and the learning techniques that work best for them, so listen closely. Perhaps most important, don't treat adult students like children; simply relate to them as people who have hired you for your support and expertise.

Reviewing and Resetting Goals

Whether your student is an adult or a child, you'll need to check in regularly about goals. Congratulate your student when she meets one of her goals, and suggest resetting them if they are too difficult or too easy to reach. Sometimes students don't notice how far they've come, so make sure to observe and articulate their progress.

Top 5 Administrative Tips for Independent Tutors

We admit "Administrative Tips" doesn't sound like the most exciting area, but believe us: a few organizational techniques will make your life as an independent tutor much, much easier. Here are Chris and Erin's favorites:

1. Make sure you store the contact information for each of your clients in one central place, ideally on a secure computer. Then you can print out copies as needed.

2. Set aside time to prepare for each session. Depending on the subject and how recently you've taught it, this might be five minutes to refresh your memory, or an hour to relearn an old subject.

3. Be sure to set time aside for regular communication, as well: when working with children, we recommend planning 55 minutes of tutoring and a 5 minute chat with the parents at the end. When you tutor adults, you can talk to them at any point in the session about how they are progressing. Also, make sure to leave time for occasional phone calls with the student's teachers or counselors, if appropriate, as described above under "Good Communication."

4. After each session, set aside five minutes to take notes and store them in a folder that is just for that student. You can review these as you're preparing for each session. They'll also be helpful if parents want to know exactly what has been covered in

recent sessions.

5. If possible, try to meet other local tutors and set up a time to share ideas; a once per month meet-up over coffee or a meal can be a great way to share stories and successful tutoring techniques. We thought it would be nice to have a place to share online, too, so log on to www.Tutoring-Expert.com/success-stories.html if you'd like to share your successes.

And, as always, here's to your continued success!

End Notes

[1] U.S. Department of Education. (1997). Evidence that Tutoring Works. Washington, DC: Office of the Deputy   Secretary, Planning and Evaluation Service, USDOE.

[2] Frerking, Beth. "Community College: For Achievers, a New Destination." *New York Times* 22 April 2007, 4A: 23.

CPSIA information can be obtained
at www.ICGtesting.com
Printed in the USA
LVHW041758221120
672387LV00003B/584

9 780984 581313